The Peasant Gourmet

The Peasant Gourmet

JONATHAN BARTLETT

MACMILLAN PUBLISHING CO., INC.

NEW YORK

COLLIER MACMILLAN PUBLISHERS

LONDON

Library of Congress Cataloging in Publication
Data
Bartlett, Jonathan, 1931-
    The peasant gourmet.

    Includes index.
    1. Cookery, International.   I.   Title.
TX725.A1B343   641.5   75-4519
ISBN 0-02-507560-8

Macmillan Publishing Co., Inc.,
866 Third Avenue, New York, N. Y. 10022
Collier-Macmillan Canada Ltd.

FIRST PRINTING 1975

Printed in the United States of America

For Elsa *and* Noah—
for entirely different reasons

Contents

Introduction

At first glance, peasant and gourmet would seem to make strange table mates indeed, but on closer inspection there is an inescapable logic to their association. Without the peasant there could have been no gourmet, as the late Alexandre Dumaine—who was considered by many to be the finest chef in France in his day—pointed out when he said that "French peasant cuisine is at the basis of the culinary art" and that everything else was simply "embellishment." In other words, those sumptuous repasts that have for so long regaled the gourmet have their origins in the solid fare served at the peasant's table, in his improvisations, his celebrations, and his ability to make do with what nature in her bounty, or lack of it, bestowed on him. Of the two, the peasant is the better bet to survive, for the gourmet is a vanishing breed—for all the bandying about we do with that overworked word.

Classically, of course, the gourmet is a person of refined and trained palate who is capable of sensing an enormous variety of subtle nuances in a canon of complex dishes and cooking styles. The tradition goes back at least to the first-century B.C. Roman epicure Lucius Lucullus, passed through Renaissance Italy, and reached its peak in Paris in the nineteenth century. It received its death blow with World War I, but like many another sturdy institution it has been a long time a-dying. It will not, however, survive much longer for three rather basic reasons. First is the appallingly high cost of food and food service, which put the epicurean restaurateur at a terrible disadvantage. (He is unable, after all, to increase the somewhat limited number of people he can serve each day without a loss of quality that would render his establishment "just another restaurant.") Second is the scarcity of chefs and other trained personnel with the skill and background to prepare and serve such meals. Finally, there is the lack of diners with the ability to discern just what the chef has done and the time and patience, not to speak of the money, to develop that discernment. (One does not become a full-fledged gourmet overnight any more than one becomes a concert pianist overnight.)

This means that the number of people capable of finding, ordering, and fully appreciating a classic gourmet meal, of chastizing the chef for shortcuts or inappropriate substitutions, and of complimenting him for new or subtle refinements or variations is small and diminishing, along with the number of those capable of providing such a meal. It is perhaps sad to see the tradition pass, but traditions have been passing for a goodly time now and very often what takes their place, while not the same, can nevertheless be highly pleasant indeed.

This brings us to the peasant. I do not mean here that downtrodden, exploited dullard whose life is chiefly extolled for being "nasty, brutish, and short," but a more idealized, perhaps, certainly more comfortable being. I am conjuring here a person imbued with the tradition of living off the land, of centuries of experimentation with the fruits of the earth as and when they become available, of determining which combinations work and which do not, of developing an entire spectrum of traditional dishes that are, of necessity, flexible, especially in their adaptability to seasonal and budgetary requirements. This ideal clearly does not confine itself to the classical Old World peasant; instead it encompasses anyone who has developed those available foods and conserved and modified them over generations, whether they be peasant, yeoman, or whatnot. Their dishes are the ones that comprise what I call the tradition of the "peasant gourmet."

Such dishes represent, in a sense, a community consensus as to the appropriate use of such foodstuffs as were to be found. They are dishes with no traceable pedigree that have evolved over generations and that vary from place to place. One example that might serve for all is cassoulet. No fewer than three French cities lay claim to "authentic" cassoulet, and even within those cities feelings run high as to whose version is acceptable and whose will rot the stomach and unhinge the reason of anyone senseless enough to try it. For the purpose of this book, all such variations are considered authentic, as are the inevitable changes that must occur in transferring a dish from one country to another. Authenticity results when the spirit of the dish is adhered to—if you are going to open a can of beans and add a pork chop and some hot dogs you have nothing that even faintly resembles cassoulet. But if you prepare the dish similar to the way it is done in its place of origin, using roughly the same ingredients—with allowances for exotics such as preserved goose that are either unobtainable or absurdly costly —you have an excellent chance of producing a dish you need not be ashamed to call by that name.

One area in which the gourmet and the peasant seem to agree—although not perhaps for the same reasons—is that the food they prepare be the best and freshest available. Fish is fresh plucked from river or stream, vegetables lovingly grown and recently picked, bread wholesome and tasty, meat properly aged, and sauces—at least in the case of the gourmet—newly prepared and never poured from a jar. Certainly these are standards to be applauded and emulated whenever possible; but they are not always feasible. In some cases they are not even to be recommended; for example, except during the season when fresh, locally grown vine-ripened tomatoes are available, it is usually advisable to substitute a good-grade can of Italian peeled tomatoes instead. They will have considerably more taste, and in this book, this substitution is generally made. As for such delicacies as lobsters and corn, which swiftly lose quality when removed from sea or stalk, few of us can have the water at the boil before setting forth to haul or pick. Obviously some compromises are necessary; the trick is to keep them to a minimum and to avoid the tricked-up, artificial, chemicalized abominations that an apparently berserk food industry seems determined to foist upon us.

A word might well be in order as to where the recipes in this book originated—in truth, from all over. Some were family recipes, others gleaned from friends, still others adapted from published ones or re-created painstakingly from meals lovingly remembered. Obviously in a book founded on traditional fare, there is little place for innovation or startling development.

And finally I must admit that books of this sort are not put together in a vacuum, for any number of other people are involved in its gestation. In some cases, I have credited the person in the recipe itself. This is done out of gratitude, not to incur censure upon him or her should something go wrong, for in many cases I have fiddled with the recipe. And in any case the responsibility for the recipes is mine. However, of all the countless others who have helped, a few deserve special mention. First of all, my wife, Elsa; my mother, Mrs. Arthur Bartlett of Essex, Conn.; my sisters, Constance Hieatt of London, Ont., and Ellen Nodelman of South Nyack, New York; Mrs. Nellie Lou Swartz of Pittsburgh, Pa., and her brood; the late Morrison Ricker; Alexander Dorozynski of Paris, France; Mary Ann Joulwan of New York City; St. Leger and Marion Lawrence of New York City; Anne-Marie Mott of New York City; James L. Steffensen, Jr., of Middletown, Conn.; Jan Wunderman of New York City; Bill York of Old Lyme, Conn.; and Alexis Lichine of New York City and Cantenac-Margaux, France. I would also like to thank all of those who tested my recipes and all who came—with who knows what degree of anticipation or dread—to try out a dish I was making for the first time. And to the patience, understanding, and critical—not to speak of gastronomical—assistance of Bruce R. Carrick—good editor, good friend—I am incalculably indebted.

New York
September 1974

1
Soups and Chowders

It is disheartening to contemplate just how many people there must be in the world for whom soup is something that comes out of a can. Not that there aren't a few laudable canned soups—the problem is that they are few, expensive, and generally not quite up to what a good soupmaker can turn out at home. As for the great mass of canned soups, they rarely rise to the level of mediocre.

The decline of soup is, of course, understandable, connected as it is to the demise of the wood-burning stove. A century ago that fine old stove was kept fired up night and day the year round, and it always had something simmering at the back. It made a lot of sense, too, for fuel was available for the bringing in and splitting, and in winter the heat it threw off combined with the cooking aromas to make the kitchen a cozy, inviting place.

To keep such a pot perpetually simmering today would be prohibitively expensive—and, given the energy crisis, probably antisocial to boot—and so a compromise is the once-a-day stock pot, to which is added the spare parts of chickens, disposable bones, vegetables that, while still good, look a bit tired for the fastidious table, and other otherwise expendable food items. The pot should be simmered for an hour or so each day. Miss a day, however, and the whole thing is apt to turn on you and then watch out!

Another alternative to the soup problem is always to keep a little stock of some sort on hand. It takes some preparation, but not much. When serving recipes that call for dis-

3

jointed chicken, for example, I buy the whole bird (it's cheaper that way) and cut it up myself in such a way that I save the back, which I then wrap in a plastic bag with the neck, gizzard, and so on, and freeze. When enough of these chicken parts have accumulated, out they come and into the soup kettle with some onions, turnips, carrots, a leek or two perhaps, bay leaf, peppercorns, a few allspice berries, and anything else that seems even remotely appropriate. Simmered lengthily and carefully strained, this yields a freezable stock that is the base for any number of soups, sauces, and stews. Not all the soups included in this section call for beef or chicken stock, but for those that do, this stock is just right.

A word about portions: when I make soup I usually plan on having plenty, either for freezing or for serving for several days. Consequently, I don't always know if I'm getting eight servings or twelve or whatever. The number of servings will also vary depending upon whether you serve the soup as a first course or as a main course. Servings, therefore, are omitted in this section.

❦

NEW ENGLAND FISH CHOWDER

Along the New England coast you can usually stir up an argument simply by asking what fish you should use in a fish chowder. Some will say cod, others haddock, and the fight's on. In truth, either one is good. I've had fine success with both, but cod—more readily accessible in most places—is my standby. If frozen cod is all that you have available, use it by all means, but be sure you have something, preferably with the bones still in, with which to make your fish stock.

1 8–10-lb. cod
1 qt. water
1 lb. salt pork
2 tablespoons butter
3 lb. potatoes
3 onions
2 qt. milk
salt and pepper
thyme

Skin the fish and take the flesh off the bones and set it aside. Don't bother being too careful—you want the fish in thin slivers, not graceful fillets. Take the fishheads, bones, and skin and put them in a large pot with about a quart of water and bring to a simmer. Let them simmer, certainly not less than an hour, while you prepare the rest of the chowder. Dice the salt pork quite fine and brown it in about two tablespoons of butter. Let it cook over a low fire, stirring it from time to time to keep it from sticking to the bottom. Peel the potatoes and cut them into small chunks. Some people dice them quite small, but traditionally they are cut into pieces about half an inch or so. Bring them to a boil in salted water until just tender, drain, and set aside. Peel and dice the onion. Add the onion to the salt pork and let it brown. Take the fish broth and strain it through cheesecloth or a muslin dishtowel. Add the cod and let it simmer for 15 or 20 minutes. Add the potatoes and pour in the onions and salt pork and bring to a boil. Add the milk and let simmer for another 5 minutes. Season, add a large pat of butter, and give it a healthy dash of thyme. Traditionally chowder is served with common crackers, but these have become uncommon now, even in New England, and so most people use pilot crackers instead. Chowder is far better the second day, therefore you should make it a day ahead of time to let it ripen.

❧

NEW ENGLAND CLAM CHOWDER

Much has been argued about the various merits of "New England" as compared to "Manhattan" clam chowder, the latter often being disdained by New Englanders as tomato soup with a clam in it. There is evidence, however, that the addition of tomatoes and other "extraneous" elements was practiced as early as Colonial days in Rhode Island, making both names misnomers. By whatever name, I prefer my chowder prepared the simpler way, and I like it better heated up the day after it's made.

3 large potatoes
¼ lb. salt pork
2 onions, diced
1 qt. clams, shucked
salt and pepper
1 pt. clam juice
1 pt. milk

Peel and cut the potatoes into cubes—not too small—and let cook in lightly salted water until not quite tender. Remove and place under cold running water to arrest further cooking. Dice the salt pork quite small and render in a skillet until crisp. Remove the pieces and let dry on paper towels. In the pork fat, cook the onions until golden. Chop the clams quite coarsely, saving any clam juice. You'll want about a pint of juice, which can be made by the addition of the bottled variety, if necessary. Strain the juice through cheesecloth or a muslin dish towel and put it into your kettle. Add the onion, salt pork, pork drippings (in which you cooked the onion), potatoes, and salt and pepper to taste and let simmer 10 minutes. Add the clams and the milk and bring just to the boil and serve. As with fish chowder, if you can find common crackers, serve them; otherwise serve with pilot crackers.

LOBSTER STEW

The lobster seems like an unlikely candidate for inclusion as peasant fare unless one calls to mind that a century ago it was exceedingly difficult to ship lobsters over long distances, that lobsters were more plentiful, and people sparser, than is true today, and that dairy products augmented the sea as a source of food along lobster-bearing coasts. Thus, the local farmer had everything at hand. A true lobster stew is composed of fresh, live Maine lobster, fresh whole milk, the kind that still has the cream on top, and the very best butter—farm butter, if you can get it. I once asked a New Englander of broad but firm epicurean persuasion if South African lobster tail might be an acceptable substitute and was coldly informed it was not. However, Maine lobster being what it is, perhaps one could try. Or use the Canadian frozen lobster. You miss such delicacies as the coral and tomalley (the roe and liver that lobster fanciers find irresistible), but the essential meat is there. This recipe should provide the essential meat for two persons.

    1 tablespoon vinegar
    1 1½ lb. lobster, alive
    ¼ lb. best available sweet butter
    1¾ pt. milk
    ¼ pt. heavy cream

Place about 3½ inches of water in the bottom of a large kettle, add a tablespoon of vinegar, and bring to a rolling boil. Firmly grasp the live lobster by the back and plunge it, head first, into the boiling water. Cover the pot and let cook almost 10 minutes. Remove the lobster, which will now be a bright red, with tongs and set aside to cool. When it is cool enough to handle, split it and remove all the meat. Set the coral and tomalley aside. Cut or pull the meat into chunks. Heat up the butter and when it begins to foam add the coral and tomalley and simmer 5 minutes. Add the lobster meat, stirring and tossing it to make sure each piece gets thoroughly covered with the flavored butter, and let cook another 5 minutes. Remove the pan from the heat and pour in the milk and cream. Bring it just to the boiling point before serving. Or better yet, let it ripen in the refrigerator and serve hot the next day.

CORN CHOWDER

This is a hearty, wonderfully inexpensive meal that should be prepared well in advance, placed in the refrigerator to ripen at least overnight, and heated up at the last minute. A fine dish for skiers, frostbite-dinghy sailors, or anyone just returning from a walk in brisk weather.

>   2 tablespoons butter
>   ½ lb. salt pork, diced
>   2½ lb. potatoes
>   1 large onion, sliced
>   2 cups chicken stock
>   1½ teaspoons salt (or to taste)
>   pepper
>   3 packages frozen corn kernels
>   1 qt. milk
>   2 teaspoons dried dill

Heat the butter in a frying pan and add the salt pork, letting it cook over low heat, stirring from time to time. Peel and cut the potatoes into 1-inch cubes, cover with water in a saucepan, and boil until just tender. Don't overcook! Drain them and put under cold running water to stop further cooking. Add the onion to the salt pork and when translucent add the stock, salt, and pepper, and let reduce slightly

over a moderate flame. Add the onions and salt pork, the potatoes, corn (still frozen, but see to it that the individual
kernels are separate), the milk, and the dill. Let simmer
10–15 minutes.

QUEBEC PEA SOUP

According to my globe-trotting, Canadian-based sister, Constance Hieatt, the keys to this are the savory ("the characteristic herb of the region") and the *whole* yellow peas.
Split yellow peas are given grudging acceptance if you can't
find the whole variety (which can be difficult!), but having
tried it both ways I would tend to favor the whole peas.
And, I suppose, in a pinch green peas might suffice neatly,
if inauthentically.

> *1 lb. dried whole yellow peas*
> *½ teaspoon dried savory*
> *1 clove garlic, peeled but whole*
> *1 bay leaf*
> *2 sprigs parsley*
> *1 sprig mint*
> *¼ lb. salt pork*
> *1 large onion, chopped*

Soak peas overnight in cold water to cover. Drain but save
the soaking water. Tie the herbs all together in a cheesecloth bag and throw all the ingredients into a heavy kettle.
Take the soaking liquid plus enough water to equal at least
6 but no more than 8 (the soup should be *thick*) cups and
bring to a boil. Simmer gently at least 3 hours. Salt to taste
and serve. According to our source, recipes that contain
such extraneous matter as carrots or ham bones are not
authentically French-Canadian. Does this mean you can't
use them? Certainly not—just don't bill yourself as Que-
becois if you do!

LENTIL SOUP

Ideally, I suppose, legumes such as peas and lentils should be cooked with the remains of a sugar- or honey-cured country-style ham, but most of us don't see such succulent and expensive delicacies all that often. So we make do with what we have, and what we have often works out perfectly well.

> 2 *cups (1 lb.) lentils*
> 1 *onion*
> 1 *celery stalk*
> 1 *carrot*
> 1 *bay leaf*
> ¼ *lb. salt pork*
> 1 *qt. chicken stock*
> ½ *lb. kielbasa, sliced in 1-inch chunks*
> *salt*
> *pepper*
> ¾ *cup cream*

Soak the lentils overnight in a quart of water. In the water in which they soaked (adding more if the water does not cover) bring the lentils to a boil with the vegetables, bay leaf, and salt pork. When it boils, reduce heat and let simmer about an hour, or until lentils are soft. Drain, removing the salt pork, carrot, and bay leaf. Put the salt pork in a large pot with the chicken stock and the kielbasa. Using a sieve or a food mill, press the lentils, onion, and celery into the stock. Heat to the boiling point and let simmer about 15 minutes. Taste for seasoning, add the cream, and serve.

MINESTRONE

I have it on the authority of Holly, Susie, and Peter that this particular minestrone really hits the spot with the younger set—as well as the rest of us. The recipe was developed by their mother, which makes it an authentic Pittsburgh minestrone. Although in my house we are not yet faced with this problem, making it looks like a splendid way to keep small fry occupied on a rainy day, assuming they're old enough to handle knives.

1 lb. white navy beans
½ lb. lean chuck, in small pieces
¼ lb. salt pork, diced
2 cloves garlic, finely chopped
3–4 onions, chopped
1 1-lb. can Italian peeled tomatoes
½ 6-oz. can tomato paste
6 pieces celery, diced
3 small white turnips, diced
4 carrots, diced
1 leek, diced
4 potatoes, diced
¼ head cabbage, shredded and diced
4 small zucchini, diced
1 teaspoon basil
½ teaspoon oregano
1 1-lb. can chick peas, drained
½ lb. macaroni
4 scallions, chopped

Unless you use the "no soaking necessary" style of beans (which you will have to do if you're going to use this as a rainy day project) soak the beans overnight in plenty of water and put them on to cook (in the same water) and simmer until tender. While the beans are simmering, brown the beef and salt pork until the beef is gray and the salt pork crisp. You can use a frying pan for this, but if you have a heavy, enameled iron pot big enough to use as a soup kettle, you can save yourself a utensil. When the meat is ready, add everything else except the beans, which are cooking, and the macaroni, scallions, and chick peas. Add about a quart of stock or water, cover, bring to a boil and let simmer over a very low flame for an hour or so. Check to make sure the meat is done (if not, simmer until it is) and if so add the beans and the chick peas and the macaroni. (You can use elbows or shells, or long, crinkly pieces of macaroni, which you can crumble into the soup.) Let simmer 10 minutes more, then add the scallions. The soup should ideally be thick enough to hold a spoon upright, but if it seems too thick, add a little more water or stock and bring to a boil.

PASTA E FAGIOLI

When I was a child growing up in New York City, the streets used to resound, and indeed may still, with various taunts and cries, not least of which was *pasta fazool*—a call that meant everything and meant nothing. It was only later that I discovered that it was not only an Italian soup but one well worth advertising on streetcorners. The name simply means pasta and beans. The pasta should be a hard (durum) wheat macaroni with no egg. It is crumbled into the soup toward the end of the cooking time. The beans are white; either great northern or white navy beans are appropriate. If you wish to be elegant, you can get imported Italian white beans, mostly from Italian grocers, but this seems like an odd dish to choose for elegance.

1 *lb. dried white beans*
2 *medium onions, coarsely chopped*
2 *cloves garlic, chopped*
2–3 *marrow bones*
6 *cups beef stock*
1 *6-oz. can tomato paste*
½ *lb. durum wheat macaroni*
1 *teaspoon rosemary*

Soak the beans in water generously to cover overnight, or in the morning if you're going to cook the soup in the evening. Then, in the bottom of your soup pot, brown the onions and garlic in olive oil until they are golden. Add the marrow bones and beans and about 6 cups of light beef stock (or water and bouillon cubes if you have no stock). Cover, bring to a boil, and let simmer, very gently, for 1 hour. When the hour is up skim off any scum that has formed at the top from the marrow bones (a tea strainer works well for this task) and stir in the tomato paste. Replace cover and let simmer 2 more hours. Add the macaroni, broken into small pieces, and the rosemary, and simmer 15 more minutes. To make an extra thick soup, just before the macaroni is added, take a cup of beans, force them through a sieve—or blend in your blender—and replace, stirring them well.

SURINAM SOUP

This soup stems from Dutch Guiana—present-day Surinam —and is about as peasanty as fare can be, and delicious in its own rough way. The salt cod and spinach help give it an almost grainy texture that is most compelling. I would not try to substitute frozen spinach for the fresh, for the pureed consistency of the frozen would, I think, not work well.

1 lb. salt cod
2 cups split green peas
2 onions
1 carrot, sliced
2 bay leaves
salt
pepper
2 cloves garlic, chopped
handful parsley, chopped
1 1-lb. can Italian peeled tomatoes, drained
1 tablespoon olive (or other) oil
2 lb. spinach

Place the cod in plenty of fresh, cold water and let soak at least overnight, changing the water once or twice. Also soak the peas in plenty of water overnight, and in the water in which they have soaked, bring the peas to a light boil. Slice one of the onions (you'll need the other later) and add to the peas along with the carrot and bay leaves. Pull the cod apart into small pieces (throwing out any bones that may be in it) and add to the peas. Let it all simmer gently until the peas are tender (maybe 1½ hours or so).

Chop the second onion coarsely, heat up the oil in a frying pan, and sauté the onion together with the garlic and parsley until the onion is soft and taking on some color. Add the tomatoes, mash them around, and let the mixture simmer another 5 minutes or so. Add a cup of broth from the peas-cod pot, salt and pepper to taste, and let the mixture simmer gently 30 minutes.

Wash the spinach thoroughly, and using only the water still clinging to the leaves, steam over medium heat in a saucepan until tender (just a very few minutes). Remove spinach, drain it, and chop it fine.

When the peas are tender, mash them and the cod through a food mill (or pop them into the blender) and return them to the soup pot. Add the spinach and the contents of the frying pan, mix it together well, and let simmer another 5 minutes, stirring from time to time. Check seasonings and enjoy.

CABBAGE SOUP

France abounds in a multitude of soups having in common some form of pork and cabbage, the cabbage being fairly ubiquitous, and pigs being relatively easy and cheap to raise. The addition of, say, a small pork shoulder would raise the protein content—and the cost—of this fine soup.

½ lb. salt pork
3 potatoes, cubed
3 carrots, coarsely chopped
2 onions, coarsely chopped
1½ pt. boiling water
1 lb. cabbage, shredded and chopped
2 cloves garlic, finely chopped
French bread

Dice the salt pork and let cook in the bottom of a heavy earthenware or enameled pot. Remove and let dry on paper towels. To the pork fat left in the pot, add the potatoes, carrots, and onions. Fry slowly, stirring constantly for 5 minutes. Pour 1½ pints boiling water over the vegetables, replace the diced salt pork, and let simmer gently for 15 minutes. Add the chopped cabbage and garlic and simmer the whole mixture for 15 minutes more. Slice the bread into half-inch-thick diagonal pieces and either brown them under the broiler (turning once and watching constantly to keep from burning) or fry them gently in a little oil. Place a piece of the bread in each soup plate and ladle the soup over it.

FRENCH ONION SOUP

To the romantic imagination, this soup conjures up pictures of revelers in Paris ending up the wee hours wandering in the hurly-burly of that great food market Les Halles, imbibing vast quantities of restorative soup. The unromantic will retort that at such a wee hour the buses and Metro will have stopped running, that taxis cost an arm and a leg, and that in any case Les Halles is no more. Nonetheless, the soup, prepared with a modicum of care, may still restore the romantic imagination.

> 2 *lb. onions*
> ½ *stick butter*
> 3 *tablespoons flour*
> 6 *cups beef or chicken stock*
> 1 *bay leaf*
> 1 *loaf French or Italian bread*
> ½ *lb. cheese (Gruyère, Emmenthaler, Parmesan, or*
>   *Cheddar) grated*
> *black pepper*
> *salt*

Slice the onions as thin as possible and separate into rings. Melt the butter in a heavy saucepan over very low heat, and when it has melted add the onions, stirring them round in the butter and let cook, still over very low heat, until onions are lightly golden but not browned. Add the flour and perhaps more butter (if it seems too dry) and let cook about 3 minutes. Heat the stock and, taking the onions off the heat, add about 1 cup to the onions, stirring furiously as you do so. Add the rest of the stock, the bay leaf, salt and pepper to taste, and return it to the flame and let cook 30 minutes at a very low simmer. Actually you could eat the soup right now, but you'd be missing half the fun. First cut the bread into slices about ¾ inch to 1 inch thick. Spread some of the cheese over the soup, then top with the sliced bread—letting it float gently. Then complete by adding the rest of the cheese over it all. Put in a 350° oven for 15 minutes. With a sturdy red wine and a green salad, this should do amply for 6 romantic revelers.

PISTOU

Here is another marvelous example of a soupy stew or stewy soup, this one from Provence, where it is made with a special variety of basil found there. Technically speaking, the pistou is not the whole soup but only the special addition at the end, which must be prepared in a mortar. Apparently, the choice of vegetables is not important so long as there are plenty of them, the fresher the better.

1 cup dried white beans
4 tablespoons olive oil
2 onions, sliced
1 1-lb. can Italian peeled tomatoes
salt and pepper to taste
½ lb. green beans in 1-in. segments
1 zucchini, unpeeled, diced
3 potatoes, peeled and diced
1 stalk celery, with leaves, diced
½ cup vermicelli
Gruyère cheese, grated

FOR THE PISTOU
3 cloves garlic
handful of fresh basil leaves or 1 teaspoon dry basil
3 tablespoons olive oil

Soak the white beans (use white kidney or pea beans) overnight in plenty of water and then simmer them in water to cover for 1 hour. Drain and set aside. In a soup kettle heat up a little olive oil and add the onion. Let it soften and change color and add the tomatoes, mashing them around with the back of a slotted spoon until they blend in. Add about 1½ pints of water and salt and pepper to taste. Bring the water to a boil and add the beans (both green and white) and the zucchini, potatoes, and celery. Let simmer 10 minutes and add the vermicelli. Now make your pistou. Pound the garlic and basil together in a mortar until they form a smooth paste. When the paste is formed, add the olive oil drop by drop, pounding constantly. When the soup is ready (when the vermicelli is done) add the pistou, stir it all around, take off the heat, top with grated Gruyère, and serve.

GARBURE

There are three points to remember about this hearty vegetable concoction from southwest France. The soup must be so thick that a ladle will stand upright in it; it must be cooked in an earthenware or enamel vessel (metal spoils the taste); and during the cooking time, the water must never stop boiling. This last requirement means that the vegetables must be at or near room temperature (heat them up if necessary) and must be added very slowly. Even in fastidious company it is polite to serve this with a red wine and to *faire chabrot* at the end. This is an ancient custom by which you pour a little red wine into the dregs of the soup in your bowl, swirl it all around, and then pick up the entire bowl and drain it, as lustily as possible. Fava beans are a large bean favored all around the Mediterranean and increasingly to be seen here. If you can find them, drop them in first, as they will need a little more cooking time than other beans. If they are not to be found, use lima beans. Dried beans can also be used, but soak them first in plenty of cold water.

2 *qt. water*
2 *tablespoons salt (or more, to taste)*
1 *lb. fava beans or lima beans, shucked*
1 *lb. string beans, in roughly 1-in. pieces*
2 *lb. potatoes, in sizable chunks*
1 *lb. carrots, in 1-in. pieces*
6 *cloves garlic*
½ *lb. green pepper, chopped*
1 *teaspoon thyme*
1 *teaspoon marjoram*
2 *lb. cabbage, chopped*
½ *lb. slab of bacon, in one piece*

Add the salt to the water and bring it to a brisk boil. Then slowly, so the water never stops boiling, add the beans, the potatoes and carrots, then the garlic and green pepper. Add the herbs and let it simmer 15 minutes, uncovered. Then add the cabbage and the bacon, cover, and let it simmer 30 minutes. To serve, remove the bacon, which is sliced separately, and ladle the soup into bowls with a spoon standing upright in each. Don't forget the red wine!

YOGURT SOUP

When cold, this Lebanese specialty makes a delightful summer lunch, a preface to a meal, or a snack. It is also good hot, but you must take care in heating it so that it stays together. It is best made with a good-quality unflavored yogurt and a homemade chicken stock. Imported dried mint seems to have more flavor than ours; but so long as some dried mint is used, it matters not where it came from.

½ cup pearl barley
1 qt. chicken broth
1 large onion, chopped
1 qt. yogurt
salt
dried mint
1 tablespoon oil, preferably olive

Soak the barley overnight in a generous amount of water, or boil it hard for 40 minutes, then drain. Bring the chicken broth to a boil, add the barley, and let it simmer until tender, 10–15 minutes. Cool to room temperature. Sauté the onion in oil until golden-brown and cool to room temperature. Bring the yogurt to room temperature. Combine all the ingredients and chill. Add salt to taste. When ready to serve, ladle out soup into bowls and taking a little dried mint between the palms of both hands, crumble it over the soup.

BESS'S BEEF WITH BARLEY

This recipe Patty Hinkley received from her mother and passed along for inclusion here. It shows its modernity by utilizing a dried soup mix, instead of doing everything from scratch, but is uncommonly good nonetheless. Just see to it that the soup mix contains mushrooms (Streit's and Goodman's come to mind as appropriate, but there are undoubtedly others I don't know about).

3½ qt. water
1 teaspoon salt
1 meaty soup bone knuckle, split
2–3 lb. meaty beef shank
1 6-oz. package vegetable soup mix with mushrooms
⅓ cup barley
2 tablespoons parsley, chopped

1 bay leaf
1 tablespoon thyme
salt and pepper to taste
3 carrots, coarsely chopped
2 stalks celery, coarsely chopped
2 tablespoons dried mushrooms

Bring 3½ quarts of water to a boil in a large soup pot and add a good teaspoon of salt. When it begins to boil add the soup bone and the beef shanks and skim as necessary. When no more scum appears, partly cover the pot, reduce the heat, and let it simmer gently for 1 hour. Meanwhile, remove the small cellophane bag of alphabets and mushrooms from the package of soup mix, empty it into about a cup of water, and set aside. Rinse and drain the rest of the soup mix. When the meat has simmered 1 hour, add the vegetables from the soup mix, barley, parsley, bay leaf, thyme, and salt and pepper to taste and simmer 20 minutes. Add the carrots and celery and simmer another 45 minutes, stirring from time to time. Drain and add the reserved mushrooms plus the additional mushrooms from the soup mix and simmer another 30 minutes. The soup is a hearty and thick one that seems to thicken dramatically and suddenly. If it seems *too* thick, add a little boiling water.

PHILADELPHIA PEPPERPOT SOUP

It has been bruited about that this soup had its origins at Valley Forge one bleak winter day in 1777–78 when General Washington wanted to cheer up the troops. The cook was unable to scrape up any food except for a mess of tripe and some pepper, and so this soup was invented. This story— unlike the soup—has always sounded pretty thin to me. It follows all too closely the story of the origin of Chicken Marengo, said to have been concocted after the Battle of Marengo at which Napoleon had beaten the Austrians so badly he had advanced well ahead of his supply wagon. His cook sent out a foraging party that came up with a chicken, some tomatoes, some eggs, some garlic, and a few crayfish, which the cook combined with some Cognac from the imperial flask. These are ingredients that might be available after a battle, and the resulting dish is apt tribute to Napoleon's undiscriminating palate (he even wanted it served again!). As to the Pepperpot, it seems unlikely that a cook would just happen on enough tripe to feed an army (literally), and even more unlikely that he could concoct of it something as good as this.

> *3 lb. tripe*
> *1 meaty veal knuckle*
> *2–3 soup bones*
> *3 onions, sliced*
> *2 carrots, chopped coarsely*
> *handful parsley, finely chopped*
> *6 allspice berries*
> *½ teaspoon thyme*
> *½ teaspoon marjoram*
> *12–18 peppercorns*
> *2 bay leaves*
> *4 qt. water*
> *4 potatoes, diced*

Wash the tripe thoroughly and cut it into 1-inch squares. Toss everything except the potatoes into a good-sized kettle, cover with about 4 quarts water, bring to a boil, and let it simmer, very gently, for 6 hours. Add the potatoes and let simmer 30 minutes more.

2
Vegetables

There is a pervasive myth in this country that most people —and all children—don't like vegetables. This has all the trappings of a self-fulfilling prophecy: if you tell a child often enough that he will not like spinach, for example, he will grow up convinced that spinach is distressing to eat. And having grown up in the habit, he will carry it with him to the grave.

But there is another reason why vegetables are frequently in disrepute and that is the way they are so often cooked. Drown any vegetable in water and boil it until all flavor and nourishment are gone and you will have a tasteless mess. Furthermore, what sadist was it that prescribed for school lunches that unholy combination of carrots and peas and compounded the atrocity by decreeing they be left to wilt on a steam table? Carrots and peas are both noble vegetables, but together they are ill matched.

Vegetable side dishes are not, however, at issue in this book, and for the purposes of this section I have added legumes (beans and lentils) as well as vegetables per se. At a time of soaring meat prices, dishes of this sort are worthy of consideration.

VEGETABLES PROVENÇALE

There are three characteristic ingredients of Provençale cooking—olive oil, garlic, and tomatoes—and so naturally all of them are used here. Depending on availability, you might want to substitute small crookneck or summer squash for the zucchini (or augment the dish by adding them). But whichever you use, don't peel the vegetable—simply scrub it well (try a dobie pad for this) and cook it skin and all. In squash season, this can be made in quantity and the excess frozen.

> *4 tablespoons olive oil*
> *4 onions, chopped*
> *3 cloves garlic, chopped*
> *2 zucchini or summer squash, cut in rounds and then cubed*
> *3 green peppers, seeded and cut in thin strips*
> *2 1-lb. cans Italian peeled tomatoes, drained, or 1½ lb. fresh*
> *½ cup dry vermouth*
> *1 teaspoon basil*
> *1 bay leaf*
> *½ teaspoon ground coriander*
> *salt and pepper to taste*

If you're using fresh tomatoes, you may want to peel and seed them. Heat up the olive oil in a large skillet, add the onion and garlic and cook until onion is limp and translucent. Add the zucchini and green pepper and let cook, stirring, 5 minutes. Add and stir in the tomatoes, then add everything else (salt and pepper to taste) and bring it to a boil. Cover the skillet, reduce the heat, and let the mixture simmer gently 15 minutes. Remove the cover, stir it all around, and let it cook, uncovered, 15 minutes more, turning up the heat slightly so that it boils actively and reduces the amount of liquid. Serves 4 as a main, more as a side, dish.

GAZPACHO

Much gazpacho these days is made, swiftly and virtually effortlessly, in the blender—an appliance that is not an unmixed blessing. The soup comes out as a homogenous syrup, which is a shame, because true gazpacho should have more texture to it—at least enough to stir up controversy whether it is a thick soup or a thin stew. So, eschewing the blender, here is a controversial gazpacho.

3 slices bread
1 2½-lb. can Italian peeled tomatoes
2 onions, finely chopped
½ cup dry red wine
salt and pepper to taste
3 cloves garlic
1 tablespoon paprika (Spanish or domestic, not Hungarian)
3 tablespoons olive oil
1 medium cucumber, in small cubes
12 black olives, pitted

Take the crusts off the bread and cut or tear into small pieces. If you are using canned tomatoes that have spices, such as bay leaves, remove any trace of the spices. Mix the onion, tomatoes, bread, red wine, and salt and pepper to taste together in a large bowl. Using a mortar and pestle, grind the garlic and paprika into a paste. Add, drop by drop, the olive oil, until the mixture has the consistency of mayonnaise. Stir in enough of the onion-tomato-bread mixture, slowly, bit by bit, until the mortar is about half full. Then pour the contents of the mortar into the balance of the tomato mixture. Add the cucumber and olives and let stand in the refrigerator at least 1 hour before serving.

EGGPLANT PIE

This is a fine, simple version of the classic Italian peasant dish, eggplant Parmigiana. It should ideally be made in an oven-proof serving dish that is higher than it is wide.

>   *1 large (2½ lb.) eggplant*
>   *olive oil*
>   *1 onion, chopped*
>   *2 cloves garlic, chopped*
>   *1 1-lb. can Italian peeled tomatoes, drained*
>   *salt and pepper to taste*
>   *mozzarella cheese*
>   *basil*
>   *oregano*
>   *handful Italian parsley, chopped*
>   *¼ cup Parmesan cheese, grated*

Peel the eggplant and cut it into even half-inch rounds, place them in a colander in the sink and put a weighted plate over them and leave for 30 minutes. Using lots of paper towels, with the heel of your hand press any excess water out of the eggplant slices. Cover the bottom of a skillet with a scant layer of olive oil and let it get quite hot. Replacing the oil as needed, fry the eggplant slices until crisp and golden on both sides and set aside on more paper towels to drain. Make sure enough oil remains to cover bottom of the pan in a very thin layer (or add if necessary) and over reduced heat sauté the onion and garlic until onion is wilted and changes color. Add the tomatoes and mash them down well with a slotted spoon. Stir and add salt and pepper to taste and add ½ teaspoon oregano, ½ teaspoon basil, and the parsley. Rub oil on your oven-proof dish, place a layer of eggplant, a layer of sauce, thin slices of mozzarella and then sprinkle a little basil and oregano over it all. Build the dish up in such layers, topping with a sauce-and-cheese layer; then evenly spread with Parmesan. Bake at 350° for 45 minutes. Serves 6.

STUFFED EGGPLANTS

The versatile eggplant comes in all sizes and has a variety of uses. This recipe is a good one for a meatless meal, for the soy flour gives you at least some protein. Two plump eggplants of about 6–8 inches in length should feed four people, especially if you're planning on serving something with it, such as a salad, for example.

2 eggplants
boiling water
1 green pepper, seeded and chopped
1 onion, chopped
1 clove garlic, chopped
oil
¼ cup soy flour
¾ cup bread crumbs
salt and pepper to taste

Cut the eggplants in half and scoop out the pulp, leaving about half an inch of shell. Put the shells in lightly salted boiling water and let water boil for 5 minutes; then remove and drain (be careful, they will be tender and limp and can puncture easily). Chop the eggplant pulp and mix it thoroughly with the pepper and onion and garlic. Heat up some oil in a frying pan and sauté the eggplant mixture over medium-low heat for 10 minutes. Add soy flour, ½ cup bread crumbs, and salt and pepper to taste. Then add enough boiling water (a cup or two) to give it a malleable but not runny consistency. Spoon it into the eggplant shells and top with remaining bread crumbs. Put a little water in a baking sheet, place the eggplants on the sheet, and bake in a 325° oven for 30 minutes.

SICILIAN EGGPLANT

According to Waverley Root's *The Food of Italy*, "Sicilian cuisine is characterized by a fondness for the sharp tang of anchovy," which explains its use in this recipe. He points out that much of Sicilian origin stems from the strong influence of the Muslims, whose culture dominated the island in medieval times. Anchovies, however, would seem to figure more because of their abundance than because of any influence stemming from the Arabian desert. Although this recipe is for two people, it is easy to expand—simply add one eggplant per two people. Just make sure the eggplants are big enough—plump ones 7–8 inches long.

> *1 large eggplant*
> *½ cup black olives, pitted and chopped*
> *2 cans long anchovy fillets*
> *1 1-lb. can Italian peeled tomatoes, drained*
> *3 tablespoons capers*
> *black pepper*
> *olive oil*

Slice the unpeeled eggplant in half lengthwise and scoop out the meat, leaving about ⅛ inch of shell (be careful not to break the shell). Bring a goodly amount of water to a rolling boil and let the eggplant skins blanch for 2 minutes, then remove carefully with a slotted spoon or tongs and set aside. Chop up the eggplant meat and mix with the olives, anchovies, tomatoes, capers, and a good grating of pepper. Moisten with olive oil, then carefully spoon the mixture into the eggplant shells and place them on a cookie sheet with a slight layer of water on it. Bake in a 325° oven for 30 minutes.

CHILI

What is the origin of chili? Mexico? The southwestern United States? I suppose this question will be debated as long, and as fruitlessly, as will the question of what goes into an authentic chili. Without trying to get into those roiled waters, I give here the chili I like to make and serve. One reason I like it is that, following this schedule, the preparation is all virtually done the day before, which makes it a good dish to serve guests. Some people cook it as briefly as 4–6 hours, others for a full 24, but if you want to cook it longer than overnight, make sure you check it every hour or so after the first 12 to see it doesn't dry out (just add a little boiling water if it seems to be getting too dry).

6 tablespoons oil
3 lb. chuck, in 1½ inch cubes
6 tablespoons sweet chili powder
6 tablespoons flour
1 teaspoon cumin
1 teaspoon oregano
3 cloves garlic, finely chopped
beef stock to make about 1½ pints
salt
pepper
1 lb. dried pinto or kidney beans

Start your preparations the night before you want to serve the dish. Heat the oil in a large, oven-proof pot with cover and toss in the meat, stirring it all around in the hot oil until it all changes color, losing its redness. Stir in the chili powder and flour and make sure the meat is well covered by them. Stir in the cumin, oregano, garlic, and a little salt and enough of the beef stock just to cover. Cover the pot and put it in a 225° oven overnight. The following morning turn off the oven (check to make sure that the water

hasn't been all used up), and in a large bowl put the beans
with generous water to cover. A couple of hours before
serving, place the beans and their liquid (add more if necessary—you want the beans just covered) in a saucepan
and let simmer 1½–2 hours. For all or part of this time you
might want to heat the oven back to 225° to reheat the
meat. When the beans are tender, drain them and mix them
with the chili and serve.

BOSTON BAKED BEANS

In New England a while back it came almost with the force
of Revealed Truth that baked beans were what you had for
Saturday night supper. There simply was no alternative.
Boston brown bread and cole slaw were the usual side
dishes, although I can recall having beet greens when the
season was right. This is the "family" recipe, sent along
from Norway, Maine by my Great-Aunt Josephine Stone,
who noted on the simmering, "I was taught by your grand-
mother to blow on [the beans] and if the skin broke then
they were ready for the oven." There are any number of
beans appropriate for baking this way, but if I had to choose
one kind, I'd make it red kidney beans.

> 2 *cups dried beans*
> 1 *medium onion*
> ½ *lb. salt pork*
> 2 *tablespoons brown sugar*
> 2 *teaspoons mustard*
> ¼ *teaspoon pepper*
> 1 *teaspoon salt*
> ¼ *cup molasses*

Wash the beans and cover them with water and about
3 inches more. Soak overnight. In the morning, simmer
slowly until the skins wrinkle—about 1 hour or so. Drain
the beans, saving the water, which should be kept good and

hot. Put the onion in the bottom of the bean pot; add the beans, making a good-sized depression in them. Wash and score the salt pork, and fit it into the depression in the beans. Mix the brown sugar, mustard, pepper, salt, and molasses and add to the beans. Add enough of the hot bean water to cover the beans, put the top on the bean pot, and bake at 450° for 3 hours and then 325° for another 4 hours. Look at the beans every hour to make sure you can see the water (adding more hot bean water as necessary) and remove the top for the last hour so that the beans won't be too wet. Aunt Jo added, "this sounds awfully complicated, but it really isn't. But it *is* an all-day operation and makes the house smell so nice and homey." Serves 6.

BEANS AND RED WINE

The "secret" here, insofar as there is one, lies in the slab bacon. The better the bacon, the more taste it will impart. I suppose regular supermarket sliced bacon could be used in a pinch, but I wouldn't expect the end result to be so tasty. The dish originally called for dried white French haricot beans, but I suspect that considerations of availability and budget will speak louder than tradition. Great northern or white navy beans would be suitable.

> *1 lb. dried white beans*
> *¼ lb. salt pork*
> *½ lb. slab bacon*
> *2 bay leaves*
> *2 cloves garlic, crushed*
> *1 teaspoon thyme*
> *2 tablespoons vegetable oil*
> *3 onions, sliced very thin*
> *1 cup dry red wine*
> *butter*

Soak the beans overnight (or all day if you're going to cook in the evening) in plenty of water. Drain and put on to cook in about 2½ pints water with the salt pork, bacon, bay leaves, garlic, and thyme. Cover and let simmer fairly vigorously for 1½ hours. Then remove the bacon and the pork, drain the beans but save the liquid. In oil, or butter and oil, sauté the onion until soft. Cut the bacon into cubes and add to the onion and let cook a few minutes. Then add the red wine and bring it to a fierce bubbling. Now add the beans, moisten with a little cooking water, and stirring it around, let it simmer gently for 10 minutes. A dollop of butter at the very end completes the dish. Serves 4–6.

BLACK BEANS WITH RUM

The ham hocks are absolutely vital to this dish, although many black bean recipes don't call for them. Some people soak the ham hocks before adding them. I don't because soaking lessens the hearty flavor that I want in the first place.

> *1 lb. black beans*
> *6 smoked ham hocks*
> *1 large onion, finely chopped*
> *2 carrots, finely chopped*
> *3 stalks celery, finely chopped*
> *2 cloves garlic, finely chopped*
> *2 bay leaves*
> *1 teaspoon thyme*
> *salt and pepper*
> *2 jiggers dark rum*
> *sour cream*

Let the beans soak in water to cover generously overnight. Remove beans, and to the water in which they have soaked, add enough water to make a total of about 6 cups. Place the ham hocks in a huge kettle and add the beans, the water, and other vegetables, the garlic, bay leaves, thyme, salt, and pepper. Bring to a boil and let simmer gently for about an hour. After the hour is about three-quarters over, preheat your oven to 350°, remove the ham hocks from the kettle (letting the beans continue to simmer) and take the meat off them. The bones, rind, and fat can be discarded. Cut the meat up small and replace it in the kettle. Remove the bay leaves. Add a hefty jigger of rum (about 1½–2 ounces). Place beans in a bean pot or dutch oven, cover, and bake at 350° until they are done, about 2 hours. Add another good jigger of rum, stir mightily, and serve with lots of sour cream. Serves 4–6.

CARIBBEAN RICE AND BEANS

Throughout the Caribbean, as in many other parts of the world, the mainstay of the diet is rice and beans—inexpensive, nutritious, filling. It is a tribute to "peasant" wisdom that even without the sausage—that traditional source of protein—rice and beans, if combined with some milk product, complement each other to provide the protein necessary for human nutrition.

1 cup red kidney beans
2 tablespoons oil
¼ lb. hot Italian sausage, chopped
pinch thyme
1 clove garlic, finely chopped
salt
pepper
1 cup raw rice
pat of butter

Soak the beans in water to cover overnight; adding more water to cover, if necessary, bring beans to a boil and let simmer until just tender; drain but save the water. Heat the oil in a large frying pan and add the sausages, letting them brown slightly, and the beans. Cook until all is browned. Add 2 cups of the bean liquid (augmented with water, if necessary), the thyme, garlic, and seasonings. When liquid simmers, add the rice and butter. Bring back to a good boil, stir it all around, reduce heat and let simmer, covered, for 20 minutes or until rice is tender and mixture is becoming dry. Serves 4.

HOPPIN' JOHN

How do certain dishes get identified with specific holidays? Turkey for Thanksgiving seems clear enough, and goose for Christmas—at least among readers of Dickens. And there may be a logical explanation for the Down East Maine custom of celebrating the Fourth of July with salmon and green peas, although I for one don't know it. But the southern U.S. tradition of celebrating New Year's Day with Hoppin' John is one of those nice ideas whose origins are as indiscernible as the name is underivable. Having been brought up in the North, I don't recall having the dish only on New Year's Day—but I do recall welcoming it whenever it appeared. If at all possible, use fresh blackeye peas; otherwise you'd better soak the dried variety overnight.

½ lb. slab bacon (unsliced)
2 cups fresh blackeye peas
1½ cups rice

Put the bacon in a large pot with about 2 quarts water and bring to a boil. Reduce heat and let simmer, gently, 45 minutes. Add the blackeye peas and simmer another 20 minutes, or until peas are nearly tender. Add the rice and let simmer another 20 minutes. Drain the peas and rice in a colander and set in a warm oven to dry out; meanwhile slice the bacon. Place the peas and rice in a bowl, top with the bacon, and season to taste. Variations on this dish include gingering it up with a little Tabasco and perhaps some chopped onion sautéed in bacon fat, and serving it with a light tomato and scallion salad dressed with oil and vinegar, all of which you mix together indiscriminately on the plate. Serves 4.

LENTILS AND KIELBASA

Kielbasa is Polish sausage and is available at most supermarkets, usually with its ends tied together to form a lopsided O. If there is a Polish butcher in your neighborhood, however, it will probably be of great benefit to get to know him, for a locally made, rather than a mass-produced, sausage will be infinitely better.

1 lb. lentils
2 tablespoons oil
4 onions, chopped
4 cloves garlic, chopped
1 1-lb. can Italian peeled tomatoes, drained
1½ lb. kielbasa, cut in half-inch rounds
1 bay leaf
salt and pepper to taste

Cover the lentils with plenty of cold water and bring them to a boil. Let them simmer about 20 minutes, then drain, saving the cooking water. In a casserole or dutch oven, heat up the oil and then brown the onion and garlic until the onions are tender. Add the tomatoes and mash them around thoroughly and let the mixture cook, stirring, until most of the liquid is gone. Add the kielbasa, stirring it around, then the lentils, bay leaf, and salt and pepper to taste. Add about half a cup of the lentil liquid, cover, and set in a 350° oven for 30 minutes. Check from time to time and if it seems to be getting dry, add more liquid. Serves 6.

LEBANESE SPINACH

It is debatable whether this belongs in a book devoted mostly to one-dish meals, but it certainly qualifies in all other respects. It should be served cold and is ideal for a quick summer lunch or snack. My only complaint is that being surrounded by spinach lovers, I can never keep it on hand.

½ cup bulgur
2 tablespoons olive oil
1 onion, chopped
1 lb. spinach, chopped fine
salt
lemon juice

Soak the bulgur in about 1 cup of cold water and set aside. Heat up the oil and cook the onion over medium heat until it is soft. Wash and add the spinach with whatever water is still clinging to its leaves and stir around until it is tender—about 5 minutes or so—and salt to taste. Drain and place in a bowl. Drain the bulgur and add it to the spinach and stir it all around until bulgur is evenly distributed throughout. Refrigerate and serve cold with a little lemon juice squeezed over it just at the last minute.

3
Poultry

Chicken at one time was considered such a delicacy that it was served only on special occasions, such as formal Sunday dinner. Then food processers discovered how to "mass produce" chickens, growing them in vast quantities and shipping them great distances in cold storage. Chicken is now relatively inexpensive as things go, and you no longer have to pluck it and then sear it to get out the pinfeathers. It does not, however, have much taste, and some of the chicken I've seen in markets has a grayish hue that bespeaks too much time in storage. There are still some good sources for chicken. The local farm is an obvious place to look, if you have one handy, and the Chinese seem to have insisted on the old standards of quality. However, in New York City's Chinatown a good chicken will cost as much as a steak—and be well worth it, too. Equally expensive (and not always reliable unless you know your source) is health-food range-fed chicken, which has the disadvantage of coming frozen. But I for one feel that for a special occasion, I will pony up the money for a "real" chicken; otherwise I'll consider the bird sufficiently versatile that I'll just make do with the best one I can get.

PAELLA

One of the classics and mainstays of Spanish peasant cooking is paella—a zesty concoction of seafood, chicken, rice, and various other additions. This one is fairly elaborate, but of course you can add or subtract as availability and budget dictate. Chorizo sausage is available canned in Spanish shops, but almost any good, garlicy sausage will be an adequate replacement. Traditionally paella is served (and indeed cooked) in the wide, earthenware paella dish, but while certainly attractive, this is by no means necessary. Any large oven-proof utensil will suffice.

2 lb. little neck clams
½ lb. shrimp
2½ lb. chicken, cut in small serving pieces
½ lb. lean pork, boneless, cubed
cooking oil
2 onions
2 cloves garlic
1 green pepper, sliced
2 large tomatoes, peeled (or 1 1-lb. can peeled tomatoes,
*   drained)*
handful of parsley (preferably Italian), chopped
1 teaspoon saffron
½ lb. chorizo sausage
4 cups rice, uncooked
1 small can artichoke hearts, drained
1 package frozen (or 1 lb. fresh, shelled) peas
salt and pepper to taste

Place clams in a deep vessel with about 5 cups water, bring to a boil, and let boil 3–4 minutes, or until all clams are open. Remove and shell the clams, saving both meat and broth. Meanwhile, shell the shrimp, place shells (not shrimp) in about 4 cups water and simmer 5 minutes or so. Combine clam broth and shrimp water. Remove about ¼ cup of the hot liquid and set the saffron to steep in it.

Brown the chicken pieces and the pork in oil and set aside. Replenish the oil, if necessary, and sauté the onion, garlic, and pepper over low heat for a few minutes. Add the tomatoes and let cook, mashing everything together and removing the tomato skins as they appear. Replace the chicken and pork. Add the parsley and the saffron with its liquid. Simmer 1 hour, or until meats are nearly tender. In 1–2 tablespoons oil, sauté the chorizo sausage and the rice until the sausage is heated through. Remove sausage and add to pot. Continue sautéeing the rice, stirring constantly, about another 10 minutes, then add to pot, stirring to make sure it is evenly mixed, and add the artichoke hearts, the clams, and the shrimp. If using frozen peas, thaw only enough so that the individual peas separate; add the peas to pot and season with salt and pepper to taste. Add additional shellfish liquid, if necessary, barely to cover. Cover the pot and simmer 20 minutes or so, until rice is tender. Serves 6.

ARROZ CON POLLO

Very simply, chicken in the Spanish style—but enough other things are added to make it a meal in itself. I feel that the real key here is the saffron, and when feeling expansive I may add more than a teaspoonful.

> *1½ cups chicken stock*
> *1 teaspoon saffron*
> *1 3-lb. chicken, cut in serving pieces*
> *¼ cup oil*
> *2 cloves garlic, chopped*
> *2 medium onions, chopped*
> *1 green pepper, chopped*
> *1 1-lb. can peeled tomatoes*
> *1 package frozen green peas*
> *1 bay leaf*
> *salt*
> *pepper*
> *2 cups uncooked rice*

Heat half a cup of the chicken stock almost to boiling and put the saffron in it to steep. In a large casserole or dutch oven brown the chicken pieces in the oil and remove the chicken. To the juices in the pan add the garlic, onion, and green pepper and sauté, stirring, until the onion is golden. At this point you can stop the preparations, if you want, and continue later. Preheat your oven to 350°. Then, to the garlic, onions, and pepper, add the chicken, tomatoes (with juice), peas (still frozen but separated), bay leaf, and remaining stock. Bring to a boil, add salt and pepper, saffron with its stock, and the rice. Stir it all together, cover, and cook in a 350° oven for 30 minutes. Serves 4–6.

CHICKEN BONNE FEMME

Alas, we'll never know whose "good lady" that bonne femme refers to, but in French cookery we all owe her a vast debt, as witness this dish. Perhaps, more than most of the recipes in this book, this one relies heavily upon the freshness and succulence of the bird selected. A fresh-killed range-fed bird is simply going to make a world of difference if compared with the usual product found at most supermarkets.

4 tablespoons butter
1 clove garlic, finely chopped
½ teaspoon thyme
juice of half a small lemon
1 3-lb. chicken
½ lb. salt pork or slab bacon
6 carrots, peeled and cut diagonally into chunks
1 lb. new potatoes
1 lb. small white onions, peeled
salt and pepper

Mash together the butter, garlic, thyme, and lemon juice and rub half of it well into the inside of the chicken. Truss the chicken. In sufficient cold water to cover, blanch the salt pork (or bacon), letting it come to a boil and simmer for a minute or two. Drain and dice it. In an oven-proof dish large enough to hold the chicken—but fairly snugly—brown the salt pork, removing the browned pieces to drain on paper towels. Rub the outside of the chicken with the remaining butter mixture and brown over low to moderate heat, quite slowly, allowing a good 5 minutes per side, for a total of 20–25 minutes. While the chicken is browning, place the vegetables in a large frying pan with 2 tablespoons butter; and coating well, let fry gently for 10–25 minutes, stirring from time to time. When the chicken is done, remove it and take out all but about a tablespoon of fat and put back the salt pork. Replace the chicken in the pot and place the vegetables around it. Salt well and grind some pepper over it. Cover tightly and heat on top of the stove until it bubbles, then place in a preheated 350° oven for about 1 hour, basting every 15 minutes or so with the liquids in the pot. Serves 4.

❦

COQ AU VIN

Chicken stewed in wine is a peasant staple of virtually every French wine-growing district, but perhaps because of the prestigious nature of the wines, the dish seems to be especially identified with Burgundy. Some food writers maintain that chicken is best cooked with one of the wines of the Touraine (from the Loire Valley). These, of course, are not always available, nor are they economical for cooking. So use what you like, so long as it's a wine you would not be embarrassed to serve at your table. Any wine you can drink—with pleasure, naturally—is good enough to cook with; any wine you can't, is not.

1 3–4 lb. chicken, cut in serving pieces
3 carrots
3 or 4 onions
2 bay leaves
1 teaspoon thyme
2 cloves garlic
1 bottle dry red wine
¼ lb. salt pork
¼ cup (approx.) brandy
½ lb. mushrooms
flour
melted butter

Take the chicken giblets (except for the liver), 1 unpeeled carrot cut in quarters, 1 onion, peeled and halved, 1 bay leaf, and ½ teaspoon thyme and place in a generous pint of water and simmer 30 minutes.

When the stock is done, strain it through cheesecloth or a muslin dish towel and discard the solids. In a largish pot, put about half a pint of the stock together with the remaining carrots (unpeeled but coarsely cut), the onions, peeled, the garlic, peeled and thwacked with a knife, the remaining bay leaf and thyme and the red wine. Bring it to a boil and then let it simmer gently half an hour or so, or until the liquid is reduced by half.

While this is cooking, put the salt pork (or bacon) in cold water, bring to a boil, and let simmer a minute or so. Remove and dice the salt pork, drying it with paper towels. Put the diced pork in the frying pan and let cook until crisp. In the pork fat, brown the chicken, taking out the pieces as they brown, and the onion. Heat up the brandy in a small saucepan and light it and pour it over the chicken, turning the pieces with a long-handled fork or spoon to keep the flames alight. Combine the chicken, wine, onions, and salt pork and simmer, gently, covered for 30 minutes. Add the mushrooms and simmer 10 minutes more.

Have some flour and some warm butter (it need not be

completely liquified) handy. Remove the chicken and all
solids from the pot and put on a serving platter, preferably
in a warm place. Work the flour and butter together into
balls the size of peas and drop them, stirring into the
sauce, over a gentle flame (don't let it boil). This will thicken
the sauce and as you stir it around you can judge if it is
thick enough for you. Pour the sauce over the chicken and
serve with fried bread or toast. Serves 4.

TURKEY MOLE

This is poultry in the Mexican style, as is shown by the inclusion of chocolate, which, like vanilla, was introduced
into world cuisine by the Indians of Mesoamerica. Just
make absolutely sure that you use the *unsweetened* chocolate. If you don't have (or can't find) tortillas, use slices of
old bread. The recipe also works for chicken, although you'll
have to scale down the ingredients to match the smaller
bird.

> *10–12 lb. turkey, cut in serving pieces*
> *1 teaspoon aniseed*
> *2 tablespoons sesame seeds*
> *6 cloves garlic, peeled*
> *¾ cup almonds*
> *½ cup peanuts*
> *½ cup raisins*
> *3 tortillas*
> *6 large tomatoes*
> *1 pinch ground clove*
> *¼ teaspoon ground cinnamon*
> *2 tablespoons salt*
> *½ teaspoon ground coriander*
> *2 oz. unsweetened chocolate*
> *2 tablespoons chili powder*
> *pepper*
> *¾ cup oil*

Place the turkey pieces in a pot and just cover it with cold water. Bring the water to a boil and let simmer 1 hour. Take all the rest of the ingredients except the oil and put them through the finest blade of your food grinder until they form a paste. Add ½ cup of oil, and heat the paste gently. It should be thick but not so thick it doesn't flow at all. If you think it too thin, simmer it for a while. If too thick, thin it with a little of the turkey water. When the turkey is simmered take it from the water and dry it (the water makes a nice stock base). In the remaining oil, brown each turkey piece thoroughly and place in a casserole. When the turkey is browned, cover it with mole sauce, cover, and let simmer 30 minutes. Serves 6.

CHICKEN CACCIATORA

This is chicken done "hunter style," but since I've never met anyone who hunted chicken, or at least admitted to it, I suppose originally it was applied to game birds of various sorts. In fact, Waverley Root, in *The Food of Italy*, cites this as a method of cooking ducks—such as widgeons and pintails— in the Venetian regions of Italy, although he omits the tomatoes and peppers. Venezia is the region that produces Italy's nicest white wine, Soave, which might be just the thing to add to this dish and wash it down with afterward.

>   *3-lb. chicken, cut in serving pieces*
>   *flour seasoned with salt and pepper to taste*
>   *4 tablespoons oil*
>   *2 onions, chopped*
>   *2 cloves garlic, chopped*
>   *2 green peppers, seeded and coarsely chopped*
>   *2 1-lb. cans Italian peeled tomatoes, drained*
>   *handful Italian parsley, chopped*
>   *1 bay leaf*
>   *½ cup dry white wine*

Dredge the chicken pieces in seasoned flour. Using a dutch oven, brown them in hot oil and when browned, remove them to a safe place. Add a little more oil to the dutch oven, if necessary, and cook the onions until they change color and become limp. Add the garlic and pepper and cook a minute or two, then the tomatoes, squashing them down with the back of a spoon. Replace the chicken, add the parsley and bay leaves, and let the whole thing simmer, covered, 15 minutes. Add the white wine and salt and pepper to taste; replace the cover and let simmer, covered, an additional 30 minutes. Serves 4.

CHICKEN PAPRIKA

The important thing here is that you must use the real imported Hungarian paprika pepper. Even paprika that simply says "imported" will not do—most of this comes from Spain and has no more zest than domestic paprika. It is fine for coloring but is useless in this dish. Real Hungarian paprika can be found in Hungarian neighborhoods and some specialty food shops. Get the sweet variety.

> *1 3-lb. chicken, cut in serving pieces*
> *2 onions, chopped*
> *2 tablespoons Hungarian sweet paprika*
> *sour cream*

Place the giblets and wingtips of the chicken in a generous pint of water, bring to a boil and let simmer 20 minutes. Strain the broth and set aside. In a dutch oven or deep casserole cook the onions until lightly golden. Add the paprika, stirring it in well and let it cook for 5 minutes. Add the chicken and let them brown on all sides. Add ½ cup of the chicken broth, cover and let simmer, as gently as possible, 45 minutes. Serve with sour cream. Buttered noodles go well with this dish. Serves 4.

CHICKEN FRICASSEE

Here's one that is quick, easy, and uncomplicated. It's certainly more appropriate to make it with chicken broth, but I was caught one time with only some fresh but quite light beef stock, so rather than use a commercial substitute I threw in the beef and it worked like a charm. The dish goes well with rice. It is not, of course, essential to use a whole chicken; chicken parts can also be used, but bear in mind they are considerably more expensive than the whole bird. This dish, fleshed out with rice and a salad, ought to take care of four people nicely.

> *4 tablespoons oil (or oil and butter)*
> *1 3-lb. chicken, in small serving pieces*
> *3 onions, chopped*
> *2 cloves garlic, chopped*
> *1 1-lb. can Italian peeled tomatoes, drained*
> *1 bay leaf*
> *2 teaspoons tarragon*
> *½ cup dry vermouth*
> *1 cup chicken broth*
> *1 tablespoon tomato paste*
> *salt and pepper to taste*

In a heavy frying pan or dutch oven, heat up a little of the oil over quite high heat and brown the chicken a few pieces at a time, removing the browned pieces and replacing them with others until all are done. Renew the oil as needed. When the chicken is done, lower the heat and add the onion and garlic and cook until onion is tender and translucent. Replace the chicken and add the tomatoes, squishing the tomatoes around. Add all of the remaining ingredients, salt and pepper to taste, bring to a boil; and over lowered heat, cover and let simmer 30 minutes, or until chicken is tender. Using tongs or a slotted spoon, remove the chicken and set aside to keep warm. Turn up the heat and let the liquid boil actively until it is reduced by half, and pour it over the chicken.

CHICKEN IN THE STYLE OF BÉARN

Béarn, in southwest France, was the birthplace of France's great King Henry IV, whose lips at birth were rubbed with a clove of garlic and a moistening of the local white wine. Béarn is hill country, rugged and independent. It is a land where pigs and geese are raised everywhere. In the fall the crop is slaughtered and much is put down, covered with lard or goosefat, as preserved pork or goose. These succulent pieces are then dredged out, dripping with fat, to be used in such specialities as cassoulet, garbure, and perhaps even this chicken, when served on extra special occasions, instead of bacon. However, a good, smoky, fat piece of bacon is an acceptable substitute. Henry IV is also the man whose aim for each French family was Sunday with "a chicken in every pot." In Béarn, this is how the chicken might be cooked.

4 tablespoons olive oil
1 3-lb. chicken, in serving pieces
3 onions, coarsely chopped
¼ lb. slab bacon, chopped
¼ cup Cognac
1 1-lb. can Italian peeled tomatoes, drained
2 carrots, coarsely chopped
2 cloves garlic
1 bay leaf
handful parsley, chopped
½ teaspoon thyme
salt and pepper to taste

In the bottom of a dutch oven heat up a little of the oil and brown the chicken, a few pieces at a time, removing the browned pieces to a plate and replenishing the oil as needed. When all the chicken is browned, remove the pieces; then brown the onion and bacon in the same utensil. Warm the Cognac. Return the chicken pieces to the dutch oven and pour the Cognac over it. Light the Cognac and keep it alight as long as you can by stirring it over the chicken with a long-handled spoon. Add the tomatoes, carrots, garlic, herbs, and wine, and salt and pepper to taste. Bring to a boil, cover, reduce heat, and let simmer gently 1 hour. Serves 4.

4

Seafood

I once knew a Norwegian who told me how, as a youngster at boarding school, he and his classmates totally disdained the fish served them once each week. "It had," he said, "been out of the water for eight hours!" Goodness knows, most of us would love to get fish as fresh as that. More and more, fresh fish is becoming something of a problem to find, except perhaps along the coasts. In much of rural New England, for example, fresh fish is almost unobtainable. And in discussing aspects of this book with friends in Pittsburgh, I was told that many of these fish dishes—and others subsequently omitted—would be virtually impossible to do there. This is a shame, for fresh fish is truly one of the great delicacies of the table and not too many fish freeze with any distinction. Squid, perhaps because it is so lean, happens to be a happy exception. Fresh fish is so much better than frozen that it is well worth the effort to obtain. Still, with the exception of clams and mussels—which I don't recall seeing frozen at all—frozen fish is certainly better than none. And in these days of high cholesterol, any fish is healthier than most of what we eat.

A word about mussels: they must be thoroughly cleaned! Authorities differ, but suggestions range from soaking them in fresh water overnight to leaving them thus for only twenty minutes to an hour or so. Roy Andries de Groot has advocated adding flour to the water (about 1 tablespoon for each 3 cups of water) and leaving them for about an hour. The mussels eat the flour avidly and purge themselves of any grit they may contain. Even then, with mussels you must scrub off the mucilaginous "beard," (a dobie pad helps); take the mussels between thumb and forefinger, squeeze from side to side to insure that the shell indeed contains a mussel and not just mud (which can happen occasionally). All this sounds unwieldy, but really it is not. If you can't soak the mussels overnight, wash them well in several waters and enjoy!

MUSSELS À LA SAL ANTHONY'S

Mussels are one of our most underused of seafoods. At one time I had a place along the coast of Maine, and when the neighbors saw a group of us gathering mussels for food, it only confirmed their suspicion that we were thoroughly mad. Prepare the mussels as described above. They can then be steamed like clams or removed from their shells to be used in casseroles or prepared as follows, as is done at Sal Anthony's Restaurant in New York City. My thanks to Anthony for giving me the recipe. You can use a prepared marinara sauce—such as Aunt Millie's—or make your own (see below).

> FOR EACH SERVING:
> *olive oil*
> *2 cloves garlic*
> *12 shelled mussels*
> *½ cup marinara sauce*
> *¼ teaspoon salt*
> *hot red pepper*
> *consommé (if necessary)*

Use a large pot with a tightly fitting lid. First pour in just enough oil to form a thin film over the bottom. Peel the garlic and give it a hefty thwack with the side of a stout knife. When the oil is good and hot add the garlic. When the garlic has turned golden add the mussels and cover the pot.

Let cook about 2 minutes, shaking the pot from time to time. When the mussels are turning colors (I peek) add the marinara sauce, the salt, and a mere pinch of red pepper. Now comes the time for judgment. If the mussels seem thin and dry, add a little consommé. If they look fat and moist, do not add consommé. Remember, when you are done you will want a pale pink, not red, sauce. When you have made your decision and the consommé has or has not been added, cover the pot again and let cook 10–12 more minutes, still shaking the pot from time to time. Serve in a deep bowl, and if you have a piece of day-old (slightly stale) French or Italian bread, throw it in too. You can substitute clams for the mussels, in which case you will have, instead of mussels à la Sal Anthony's, Clams Posilippo.

MARINARA SAUCE

4 tablespoons oil (preferably olive)
2 onions, chopped
1 clove, garlic, chopped
2 1-lb. cans Italian peeled tomatoes, drained
¼ cup dry red wine
salt and pepper
½ teaspoon oregano

Heat the oil and cook the onion and garlic until onions are soft. Add tomatoes and wine and let cook over high heat 5 minutes. Reduce heat and let simmer 1 hour. Add salt, pepper, and oregano, stir briskly.

MUSSELS RISOTTO

The one refinement I have added to this adaptation of an old Italian staple is clam juice instead of chicken broth; but because not everyone likes the richer flavor the clam juice gives, you may want to use chicken broth. The mussels should be cleaned according to the instructions on pages 55–56. Imported Italian risotto is elegant (and expensive) but ordinary long-grain rice suffices nicely.

> *4 lb. mussels (in shells)*
> *2 cups dry white wine*
> *1 cup onion, finely chopped*
> *2 cloves garlic, finely chopped*
> *2 tablespoons butter*
> *2 cups rice*
> *¼ cup Italian parsley, chopped*
> *salt and pepper*
> *clam juice (or chicken broth, if you prefer)*
> *Parmesan cheese*

Steam the mussels in 1 cup white wine until they are all opened—no more than 10 minutes. Taking out 1 open mussel for each person, shell the remaining mussels and save mussels and juice. In a large pot with a cover, cook the onion and garlic in oil and butter until onion is limp. Add the rice and cook, stirring, over a low flame for 2 minutes. Add the parsley, 1 cup of wine, salt and pepper and let cook 2 more minutes. Through cheesecloth or a muslin dish towel, strain the mussel liquid into a measuring cup and add clam juice (or chicken broth) to make 3½ cups. Add it to the rice and let simmer 25–30 minutes. About 5 minutes before rice is ready, stir in the mussels, sprinkle with grated cheese, and place the unshelled mussels over the top. Serves 6.

MUSSELS MARINIÈRE

This may indeed be the most common method of cooking mussels, and of course there are any number of variations. Do you steam the mussels in water or in wine? Do you reduce the cooking liquid prior to replacing the mussels? In truth, almost anything goes.

2 *lb. mussels*
dry white wine
1 onion, chopped
2 cloves garlic, finely chopped
handful parsley (Italian, by preference) chopped
salt
pepper

Clean the mussels, as described on pages 55–56, and place them in a large pot or kettle with about an inch of white wine. Bring to a boil and let boil 5–10 minutes, or until all the mussels are open. Remove the mussels and strain the broth through cheesecloth or a muslin dish towel. Clean the pot. Pour the strained stock back into the pot and add the onion, garlic, parsley, about ½ cup more white wine, a pinch of salt and a good grinding of black pepper. Replace the mussels and stir it all together. Bring to a boil and, reducing the heat, let it simmer gently 10 minutes. Serve with chunks of crusty French bread to sop up the juices. Serves 4.

PROVINCETOWN CLAM PIE

Why this should take its name from the town on Cape Cod's outer edge I do not know—perhaps it was collected there. Use little neck or cherrystone clams and you can even buy them shucked if you wish.

1 qt. clams, shucked
¼ lb. salt pork
1 pint flour
½ teaspoon baking soda
1 teaspoon baking powder
1 scant teaspoon salt
½ cup butter
½ cup lard
milk
salt and pepper

Chop the clams, cover them with water, and let cook 10 minutes. Drain, but save the liquid. Dice the salt pork and let cook in a frying pan until crisp, then add to the clams. Mix together the flour, baking soda, baking powder, and salt. Mix the butter and lard. Then, a little at a time, cut the butter and lard into the flour mixture, adding a little milk as needed. Divide the dough into halves and roll out. Line the bottom of a pie pan with the dough and put in the clams. Add several dots of butter, salt and pepper, and moisten with a little of the clam liquid. If the liquid seems too thin, add a touch of flour to it. Add the top crust, cut several incisions in the top, and bake in a 325° oven for 1 hour. Serves 4.

SPANISH FISH STEW

Many people are put off by such delicacies as squid and eel, which is unfortunate for they add a wonderful authority to a dish like this. Leaving them out would be like listening to Handel's *Messiah* sung by a chorus in which there were no basses. Having said that, I will admit that eel is so hard to find that I often do leave it out, but leaving out both squid and eel would be to do this dish a vast disservice. The paprika used here is the mild domestic or Spanish, not the true Hungarian paprika pepper. You can use a Spanish wine if you like, but as Spain is not renowned for its white table wines, I wouldn't make a point of it. Any decent dry white wine will do.

> 12 *little neck clams*
> 24 *mussels*
> 1 *cup dry white wine*
> ½ *teaspoon saffron*
> 3 *onions, coarsely chopped*
> 2 *green peppers, coarsely chopped*

3 cloves garlic, coarsely chopped
½ lb. baby squid (or octopus), chopped
½ lb. eel, boned, skinned, and chunked
½ lb. cod fillets, chopped in large pieces
1 1-lb. can Italian peeled tomatoes
2 bay leaves
1 teaspoon paprika
½ teaspoon thyme
pinch of salt
a grind of pepper
¼ cup Italian parsley, chopped
½ lb. medium shrimp

Wash the mussels and clams thoroughly in several waters. In a tightly lidded pot, steam the mussels in ½ cup of white wine until they are opened. Shell the mussels and set aside. Set the saffron in a quarter of a cup of hot water to steep. In a large coverable pot sauté the onion, pepper, and garlic in oil until the onions are limp. Add the squid, eel, and cod and sauté gently for a couple of minutes—until you get a splendid fishy aroma. Add the tomatoes, wine, saffron (with its water), spices, and parsley and simmer, gently, uncovered 10 minutes. Cover and simmer 10 minutes more. Add the shellfish, stirring in the mussels and placing the clams around the top, and cook another 5–10 minutes, or until clams are open. Serves 6.

LIGURIAN FISH STEW

The Ligurian seacoast, with its great seaport of Genoa, is renowned for its herbs, especially basil. Sailors have spoken of offshore breezes wafting the scent of basil and thyme through the unpolluted air to the homeward bound seafarer, inducing a frenzied appetite. The following stew is the kind of thing you might find on that coast, although I must admit I have never heard of the mackerel being a Mediterranean fish. It simply happens to be convenient where I live.

> *3 tablespoons olive oil*
> *4 onions, finely chopped*
> *2 large carrots, finely chopped*
> *3 stalks celery, finely chopped*
> *handful parsley, finely chopped*
> *3 cloves garlic, finely chopped*
> *2 tablespoons basil*
> *salt*
> *pepper*
> *1½ lb. mackerel, cleaned and with head and tail*
> *   removed*
> *½ cup white wine*
> *12 clams, well scrubbed*

In about 3 tablespoons olive oil over medium high heat cook the vegetables, basil, and salt and pepper to taste for a good 5 minutes or more. Slice the mackerel (bones and all) into 1-inch pieces. When the onions *et al.* are well blended, add the mackerel and white wine, top with the clams, cover and let simmer about 15 minutes, or until clams are open. Serves 4–6.

BRANDADE DE MORUE

This is a Provençale speciality, which seems odd because the cod is not a Mediterranean fish and salt fish would hardly seem what one would expect of those to whom all the riches of Mediterranean seafood are available. Notwithstanding, salt cod is enjoyed and prepared in a number of ways throughout southern France and Italy. To make this dish you must have a mortar and pestle, a strong arm, and a certain amount of patience. The results are worth it, especially if you use a good imported virgin olive oil (i.e., from the first pressing). Also try to pick out a piece of salt cod that is plump and white.

> 2 *lb. salt cod*
> 2 *cloves garlic*
> 2 *cups olive oil*
> 2 *cups milk*

A couple of days before you make this dish, soak the cod in cold water, changing the water from time to time. Drain it, place it in a saucepan, cover it with fresh cold water and bring it to a boil. Let it simmer about 10 minutes. Drain it, and flake it, removing any pieces of skin or bone. Now the work starts. Put the fish and the garlic in your mortar and with the pestle grind it into a paste. About the time you think it's pasty enough, you've probably just begun. Keep at it and make it as smooth as possible. Place the oil and the milk in separate saucepans and keep them just barely warm (I find that putting them over the pilot light of my gas stove keeps them about right). With a long tablespoon, put alternate spoonfuls of milk and of oil into the fish, grinding more after each addition. Keep this up until all the oil and milk is gone. The fish should now have the consistency of very heavy cream. Serve on fried bread or toast. Serves 4.

STEWED SALT COD

This is an example not only of the ubiquitous cod but also of the ubiquitous codfish stew. John Hess, whose thoughts on food enhanced *The New York Times* for a too-brief period, found the recipe in the legacy of an Italian family. Beulah Fredericks, on the other hand, remembers it from her youth in Trinidad. Whatever its provenance, it makes an interesting—and tasty—variation to the menu.

> *1 lb. salted cod*
> *3 medium onions, sliced thin*
> *2 green peppers, chopped*
> *3 cloves garlic, minced*
> *olive oil*
> *2 1-lb. cans Italian peeled tomatoes, drained*
> *1 bay leaf*

Soak the cod in plenty of cold water for a day or so before you make the dish, changing the water from time to time. Take the onions and pepper and garlic and sauté them in oil over medium heat until the onion is limp. Add the tomatoes, mashing them with the back of a large spoon; add bay leaf and let all simmer together. Drain the fish and shred it, discarding any pieces of skin or bone. Add all the cod and stir mightily, mixing it all together and simmer for 10–15 minutes. Serves 4.

❦

FISH HUNGARIAN STYLE

The distinguished psychologist Vera John cooked this one evening and told of how, as a child, she would be taken on a trip down the Danube on Sundays, the trip culminating in a visit to a small country inn where this dish was served. I may have taken a few liberties with her preparation, but I trust the end result is still properly Hungarian. The one liberty that would instantly remove this from the Hungarian repertoire would be to use ordinary paprika instead of the true, authentic Hungarian paprika pepper. Hungary is, of course, a landlocked nation, and the fish used there would be river fish. In most of the United States ocean fish are easier to get, and so any (or any combination of) the firm-fleshed fishes should do, such as striped bass or bluefish or even cod.

> 3 *lb. assorted fish, with trimmings, cut into thick*
> *chunks*
> 3 *tablespoons butter*
> 2 *onions, chopped*
> 1 *1-lb. can Italian peeled tomatoes, drained*
> 2 *tablespoons paprika*
> 2 *green peppers, chopped*
> *salt and pepper to taste*
> *sour cream*
> 3 *cucumbers, sliced thin*

Put the fish trimmings (heads, tails—everything but innards) in a quart of water and bring to a boil. Reduce heat and let simmer 30 minutes. Strain the broth and set aside. In a heavy pot with a cover, heat up the butter and add the onion and tomatoes; cook slowly for 5 minutes. Then add the paprika, slowly, a little at a time, just adding enough to make the mixture a delicate orangy-red. Add the fish and a little fish stock and simmer gently 20 minutes. Remove the fish and place in a warm place. Add the green pepper to the liquid, cover, and let simmer, somewhat more vigorously, 15 minutes. Replace the fish and serve with a dollop of sour cream on top, and on the side, very thinly sliced cucumbers dressed with the following:

CUCUMBER DRESSING

> 1 *teaspoon sweet paprika*
> ¾ *cup cold water*
> ¼ *cup vinegar*
> *pinch salt*
> *pinch sugar*
> *pinch pepper*

VATAPA

This is a speciality of the Brazilian coastal city of Bahia (now called Salvador), which was the confluence of Portuguese and black African culinary influence in Brazil. Black slaves did the cooking using both Portuguese and native South American ingredients. Vatapa is not suitable if you want a quick meal. I consider it a weekend dish, for the preparation will consume a good part of the day in laying out the ingredients in small covered dishes in the order in which they are added. Some of the ingredients can be a problem, especially the dried shrimp, the dende oil (a rich, orange-colored palm-tree oil), and perhaps the hot chilies. Obviously, living near a Brazilian grocery would be ideal, but lacking that you can find dried shrimp in Chinese groceries. Mexican and Italian markets often have suitably hot chilies. If you can't lay your hand on dende oil, use olive oil (Craig Claiborne, writing of this dish in *The New York Times*, suggested adding a tablespoon of paprika to the olive oil) or perhaps African palm kernel oil.

> *1 coconut*
> *½ lb. dried shrimp*
> *6 tablespoons olive oil*
> *4 onions, chopped*
> *1 clove garlic, finely chopped*
> *1 green pepper, seeded and chopped*
> *4–6 hot chilies*
> *1 1-lb. can Italian peeled tomatoes, drained*
> *1½ cups yellow cornmeal*
> *1 cup water*
> *1 lb. fresh shrimp*
> *1 lb. fresh fish (cod or similar fish is fine) boned and*
> *   cut in 1-in. pieces*
> *½ cup dende oil*

1 cup peanuts or cashews
1 tablespoon coriander
salt
pepper

First prepare your coconut, cracking it but saving the milk. Then grate it, spreading the gratings on a cookie sheet, sprinkling with moisture, and allowing to warm up in an open 250° oven; place the gratings in a strong cloth or muslin dish towel and squeeze out as much moisture as possible. When dry, place the gratings in a pan with 3 cups of water, bring to a boil, and simmer 10–12 minutes. Combine all the liquids and discard gratings. (An alternate procedure with the coconut is to peel off the brown rind from the cracked and husked nut with a potato peeler, slice meat thin, and put in electric blender in the approximate proportions of ½ cup coconut and ¼ cup warm water. Blend and save water. Both methods will give the requisite liquid—it just depends upon which you like least, grating the coconut or peeling it.)

Soak the dried shrimp in plenty of water overnight. In a large, heavy-bottomed pot, heat up the olive oil and add the onion and garlic and let brown slightly. Drain the dried shrimp (saving the water) and add together with the green pepper and chilies and cook 3–5 minutes, stirring; then add the tomatoes, raise heat and cook another 5 minutes. Add about 2½ cups of water the shrimps soaked in, cover, bring to boil, reduce heat, and let simmer 30 minutes. With a potato masher, mash everything in the pot until it's all a mush. Slowly add the cornmeal, stirring furiously as you do so (a wire whisk is good at the outset, but as the mixture thickens, you'll probably want to switch to a wooden spoon). Keep stirring about 20 minutes. The mixture will get as thick as bread dough as you roll it around in the pot. Add 2 cups coconut milk and the cup of water and stir it all around as a sort of a paste. Gently stir in the fresh shrimp and other fish, and simmer 10–15 minutes. Stir in the oil (dende or olive) and add nuts, coriander, salt, and pepper. Bring to a boil and remove from heat. Serve with rice, for 6 people.

FISH HASH

I once made this in the middle of Maine's Penobscot Bay on a sailboat. We had baked a couple of good haddocks the night before and plenty was left over. As the day began with no wind whatsoever and no apparent reason to think wind would ever appear, I braved the jeers of the crew ("Who ever heard of *fish hash?*") and went below. The obvious happened: the wind came whistling in about midway through the cooking and the hash damn near ended up on the cabin ceiling. It was salvaged, however, and even those crew members most skeptical of the dish asked for seconds.

> 2 *cups cooked fish*
> 4 *potatoes (Maine or Long Island—not Idahos)*
> 2 *onions, coarsely chopped*
> *butter or oil*
> *salt and pepper to taste*

Pick over the fish with the greatest of care, shredding it and removing *all* bones. Peel the potatoes and let them boil in water to cover until just soft, then remove and place in cold water to keep them from cooking too much. Dice them. Sauté the onions over medium heat in oil until they are limp. Mix together the fish and potatoes and onion and season to taste. Put about 4 tablespoons of butter and oil into a frying pan and let it heat up. Then spread the hash evenly over the pan and cook, gently, for 15–20 minutes, or until a good crust forms on the bottom. Serves 4.

SQUID GENOA STYLE

Squid is another of our neglected forms of sea life, but people of Mediterranean origin—especially Italians and Greeks—know just how good it can be. It may be a challenge to obtain squid outside the large coastal cities. I'd try an Italian or Greek fishmonger (if you have one nearby) or, failing that, ask the local fish store (or even supermarket) if they can get it for you—ask for *baby* squid. Squid is obtainable frozen, and no violence is done to it in the freezing process. For those with worrisome arteries, squid happens to be extremely low in cholesterol.

> 2 *lb. baby squid*
> 3 *onions, chopped*
> 3 *tablespoons oil*
> 2 *tablespoons parsley, chopped*
> 2 *cloves garlic, finely chopped*
> ½ *lb. fresh mushrooms, sliced*
> ½ *teaspoon rosemary*
> ½ *teaspoon basil*
> 1 *1-lb. can peeled tomatoes*

Clean and wash the squid and cut into 1-inch squares. (The tentacles are most easily cut with scissors.) Brown the onion in the oil until nearly golden. Add the parsley, garlic, mushrooms, rosemary, and basil. Let cook over low-to-medium heat for 5 minutes. Add the squid and the tomatoes (with liquid), mashing the tomatoes until they are mushy. Cover and let simmer for about 45 minutes or until squid is tender but still very slightly chewy. Serves 4.

5
Meat

We are all, goodness knows, familiar with steaks and chops and roasts, and there are few of us who can't grill a hamburger or prepare a hotdog. Such standards will not, consequently, be included here. Instead, I have tried to include various ways of combining various meats into meals that have given pleasure, and nourishment, to countless millions over the ages. The dishes run the gamut from the familiar—such as lamb stew—to what must be to Western eyes, anyway, exotic—such as couscous, which I consider one of the best of all possible dishes for a large party.

POT AU FEU

This is a long-time family favorite, particularly in cold weather. If the market seems to have better parsnips than turnips, they make a fine substitute, or—if you're feeling flush—augmentation. Some recipes call for cabbage (usually removing some broth to cook the cabbage in separately) and others may add potatoes or salt pork. A soup bone or veal knuckle, if you can lay your hands on one, would certainly enhance the richness of the broth. If I had to make a choice between making this with beef or making it with fowl, I would choose beef.

3–4 lb. piece of chuck
5 qt. water (approx.)
4 whole leeks, tied together with string
6 carrots, scraped
4 small white turnips, peeled and quartered
2 large onions, peeled and stuffed with 2 cloves each
2 bay leaves
10–12 peppercorns
3–4 lb. fowl
1 teaspoon thyme
parsley

Tie—or have tied—the beef firmly and place in the water in a large vessel and bring to a boil. Lower heat and let it simmer, removing any scum that forms on the top (a small tea strainer works well for this). When the water becomes clear, add the vegetables, the bay leaves, and the peppercorns. Let simmer—very gently—3 hours, covered. Add the fowl and simmer not more than another hour. Fifteen minutes before dish is done, add the thyme and a handful of chopped parsley. When serving, discard the leeks and place the meat and chicken—which will doubtless be falling off its bones—on a platter. Surround with the vegetables, strain the soup through a muslin dish towel, and serve in a separate bowl. Lots of French bread and a green salad make a fine accompaniment. The excess soup can be used later in the week. In my house, there is seldom any leftover soup. Serves 6.

BEEF EN DAUBE

The word *daube* is derived from an Italian word meaning "cook," which would cause one to believe that the title of the dish simply means "cooked beef." There are, of course, innumerable ways of cooking beef, but the variations on *beef en daube* probably only run into the thousands. Here is one.

3½ *lb. chuck*
2 *carrots*
2 *onions*
2–3 *small turnips*
8 *cloves garlic*
½ *cup vinegar*
¼ *cup olive oil*
4–5 *bay leaves*
½ *teaspoon thyme*
½ *teaspoon oregano*
6–8 *peppercorns*
dash Cognac, or other brandy
white wine
½ *lb. slab bacon*
butter and/or oil
1 *cup beef stock*
1 *1-lb can Italian peeled tomatoes, drained*
1 *small can anchovies*

Cut the beef into roughly 1-inch cubes. Peel and chop coarsely the carrots, onions, and turnips, and peel and smash the garlic. Combine in a large bowl with the vinegar and oil, 2 bay leaves, the thyme, oregano, 6–8 peppercorns, dash brandy, and enough white wine to cover and leave overnight. Remove from marinade and dry each piece of beef separately and completely. (This will take a large amount of paper towel.) Blanch the bacon for a minute or two in rapidly boiling water. Remove, but keep, the bacon rind. Slice the bacon into thin strips and cut the rind into small squares.

In a large oven-proof casserole, brown the bacon and rind in butter or oil, or in oil and butter, and set aside on paper towels to drain. Brown the beef, a little at a time, and set aside. When all the beef has been browned, return it all to the casserole and mix in the bacon and bacon rind. Add 1 cup of the marinade liquid and 1 cup beef stock. Add the vegetables from the marinade (taking care to remove the old bay leaves). Add tomatoes, 2 new bay leaves, and the anchovies, ground to a paste. Stir all together and when it comes to a boil, cover and place in a 350° oven for 3 hours. Serves 6.

PROVENCALE BEEF STEW

Throughout Provence the olive tree abounds, its gnarled branches taking on macabre configurations, its fruit being eaten as is or used in cooking or pressed into valuable olive oil. In addition to olives, the other indispensible ingredients of most Provençale cookery are garlic and tomatoes. All are used in this dish.

olive oil
¼ lb. salt pork, diced
3 lb. chuck, cubed
3 onions, sliced
½ cup dry red wine
1 1-lb. can Italian peeled tomatoes, drained
½ cup beef stock
3–4 strips orange peel
2 cloves garlic, mashed
2 bay leaves
1 teaspoon marjoram
1 teaspoon thyme
pinch saffron
salt
pepper
12 green olives, pitted and halved
13 black olives, pitted and halved

In a large, heavy casserole heat up a little olive oil over a high flame and brown the salt pork, removing it as it gets brown and placing the pieces on absorbent paper. In the fat, brown the beef a few pieces at a time and remove as they get brown. Remove all but about 1 tablespoon of the fat and brown the onions until they are wilted and translucent. Then add the wine and replace the beef and salt pork. Add the tomatoes, stock, orange peel, garlic, and spices and bake in a 350° oven for 1½ hours. Place the olives in a sieve and lower them into a pan of rapidly boiling water for 5 minutes. Remove, let drain a moment, then add to the stew and cook 1 additional hour. Serves 6.

BEEF BOURGUIGNONNE

What is there to say about this dish that hasn't been said a million times? Most simply it is beef cooked with bacon and vegetables in a red wine sauce that at the end is thickened with butter and flour.

> 2 lb. lean stewing beef, cut in approx. 1-inch cubes
> 1½ cups dry red wine (a Burgundy would seem
>   appropriate)
> oil
> 2 onions, chopped
> salt
> pepper
> 2 bay leaves
> ½ teaspoon thyme
> ½ lb. slab bacon
> 2 large carrots, chopped
> 3 leeks (white part only) chopped
> 2 cloves garlic, finely chopped
> handful of parsley, chopped
> ¼ cup Cognac
> butter
> 1 tablespoon flour
> ½ lb. mushrooms, sliced

The night before you're going to cook this (or perhaps the morning of the day) put the meat in a large bowl with the wine, 1 tablespoon of oil, 1 large onion, sliced, salt, pepper, 1 bay leaf, and a pinch of thyme and let marinate. When ready to go, strain the marinade keeping the onion or not as you wish (I do), and discarding the herbs. In a heavy oven-proof pot, heat up a little oil and brown the meat, a few pieces at a time, over high heat, and remove. When this is done, slice the rind off the slab bacon (but keep it) and dice both bacon and rind. Place both in pot, which should be quite dry, and add the other onion, carrots, leeks, garlic, and parsley and sauté—over low-to-moderate heat —until the bacon is cooked and the vegetables are lightly browned, stirring from time to time. Add the beef and give another stir. Add the marinade liquid and the Cognac. If this is inadequate to cover—just—the stew, add a little beef stock (MBT and George Washington are standbys in my kitchen). Add bay leaves and thyme, cover, and bring to a simmer. Place the whole thing in a 350° oven and leave it there for 1 hour. In the meantime, soften a little butter and with the flour make balls—the size of peas—of butter and flour. When the stew has cooked its hour, remove it and add the "peas," stirring as you do so, until the stew seems to be of an acceptable consistency or until you get bored. Then add the mushrooms and replace the cover. Return to oven for 2 more hours. A good crusty French bread makes a delicious accompaniment. Serves 6.

VEAL RAGOUT

It's a shame that so much of the veal available in this country is either mediocre in quality or outrageously expensive. Often it's just plain tough, but long cooking will generally overcome that. So simmer this for a greater or lesser time, depending on what veal you have available.

3 lb. veal shoulder, boneless
oil or butter
4 yellow onions, sliced
1 cup stock
1 cup dry white wine
1 teaspoon tarragon
4 cloves garlic, finely chopped
2 bay leaves
1 1-lb. can Italian peeled tomatoes, drained
1 lb. small, white onions
4–6 small carrots
2 lb. new potatoes
1 package frozen peas

Cut the veal into cubes and brown in oil or butter in a frying pan. Meanwhile, brown the yellow onions in oil or butter in a large utensil for which you have a cover (but don't put it on yet). Remove the veal as it gets brown, and when it is all done, deglaze the veal-browning pan with the stock and pour it all over the onions, which should be golden-brown. Then add the veal, wine, spices, and tomatoes to the onions, mix it all together and then cover and let simmer slowly for 1½–2 hours.

Peel the white onions; scrape and quarter the carrots and cut them into 1½-inch lengths; wash the potatoes and cut them into uniform shapes about the size of the smallest. Add the onions, carrots, potatoes, and frozen peas to the stew about ½ hour before you're ready to serve it and let them simmer with it. Serves 4.

CARBONNADE FLAMANDE

This Belgian dish is a stew of beef cooked in onions and beer (which evaporates during the cooking process leaving an incomparable richness and flavor). One source reports that it is traditionally made with equal parts of onions and beef, which sounds tidy but overbalances the dish. Lager beer is workable, but dark beer is much to be preferred and stout, it says here, is far and away the best.

butter (or butter and oil) for browning
3 lb. chuck, in 1-in. cubes
2 lb. onions, sliced
3 cloves garlic, finely chopped
1 cup beef stock
1 bottle stout
1 teaspoon thyme
parsley or celery tips
1 teaspoon sugar
1 tablespoon vinegar

In a little butter (or butter and oil) brown the meat over high heat and remove from pan. Lower the heat and slowly (about 20 minutes or so) cook the onion and garlic until golden. Replace the meat and add the stock, beer, herbs, sugar, and vinegar and, stirring once, cover and simmer until tender, about 2½ hours. Serves 6.

ESTOFADO

Here is a delicious recipe from friends who have recently spent a good deal of time touring Spain. It is a Spanish meat stew (lamb would probably serve as well as beef). The apricots and currants suggest an Islamic influence. There are some good red table wines from Spain—the best is Rioja—which would be appropriate to serve with this (and to make it with), or a decent California red might suffice—a Zinfandel, for example.

½ cup currants
½ cup dried apricots, cut in half
¼ cup oil

2 *lb. lean chuck, cubed*
2–3 *onions, peeled and sliced*
2 *green peppers, seeded and cut in thin strips*
3 *cloves garlic, finely chopped*
2 *cups dry red wine*
2 *1-lb. cans Italian peeled tomatoes, drained*
salt and pepper to taste
2 *teaspoons dried basil*
2 *teaspoons dried thyme*
2 *teaspoons dried tarragon*
3 *bay leaves*
½ *lb. mushrooms, sliced*
½ *cup black olives, pitted and sliced*
1 *tablespoon flour*
1 *cup cold water*

Soak the currants and apricots in warm water to cover.
Over a hot fire, pour a little oil in a skillet and brown the
chunks of meat a few at a time, removing them as they are
done and replenishing the oil as necessary, but using as little
as possible. When they are done, lower the heat and add the
onion, pepper, and garlic and let sauté, stirring, until onions
are limp. Drain the currants and apricots. To the onion mixture, add the meat, currants and apricots, wine, tomatoes,
salt and pepper to taste, and herbs; cover, reduce heat, and
simmer 1 hour. Add the mushrooms and olives and simmer
30 minutes longer. Stir the flour into the water and add to
the stew, stirring constantly until it thickens and bubbles.
Serve with rice and a green salad, for 4 people.

BEEF AND KIDNEY PIE

In the "good old days" when people who could afford to eat
could afford to eat well, oysters were routinely added to beef
and kidney pie not only in England but New England as

well. Although they add a subtle extra dimension, oysters also add a not very subtle extra cost, and thus can be left out with impunity. You can also substitute veal for the beef, if you wish. Use lamb or veal kidney if possible but if all that's available is beef kidney, let it soak for 2 to 3 hours in 2 cups water to which you have added 3 tablespoons vinegar.

1½ lb. chuck
flour (for dredging)
2–3 onions, chopped
2 tablespoons butter
beef stock
¾ lb. kidney
½ lb. mushrooms, sliced
12 oysters, shucked
1 bay leaf
salt and pepper to taste
nutmeg
pie crust

Cut beef into cubes of about 1 inch or so and dredge in flour seasoned with salt and pepper. Cook the onions in butter until lightly golden. Add the beef, a few pieces at a time, and brown, removing when browned. When all the beef is browned, replace in casserole and add beef stock to cover. Cover and simmer 1 hour. Remove any membranes from the kidneys, wash thoroughly, and slice thin. Brown quickly in butter over a medium-high fire. When the hour is up, add the kidney, mushrooms, oysters, and seasonings to the beef and let simmer another half hour, or until beef is tender. Remove cover and place pie crust over top of pot in its place. Put in 450° oven for 20 minutes, or until crust is browned. Serves 4–6.

NOTE: Prepare a standard pie crust, enough to fit over top of cooking pot. However, instead of regular shortening, use diced beef suet, which will give the crust a more hearty flavor.

OXTAIL CASSEROLE

When we think of animals' tails we think of small wispy things; but then our beef critters are neither small nor wispy, so why should their tails be? In fact, there is a lot of meat on an oxtail, and mighty good at that.

> *seasoned flour (whole wheat, preferably)*
> *4 lb. oxtails*
> *oil*
> *beef stock*
> *dry red wine*
> *2 lb. onions, peeled and halved*
> *2 lb. potatoes, peeled*
> *4 large carrots, coarsely sliced*
> *¼ lb. mushrooms*
> *3 leeks (white part only)*
> *3 cloves garlic, peeled*
> *10–12 peppercorns*
> *10–12 allspice berries*
> *½ teaspoon sage*
> *salt to taste*

Season the flour with a little salt and pepper. Make sure the oxtails are good and dry and dredge them in the flour, then brown in oil in a large casserole. When well-browned, drain off excess oil and add beef stock and red wine in equal parts barely to cover. Add the onions, potatoes, carrots, mushrooms, leeks, garlic, peppercorns, allspice, sage, and salt. Cover and cook in a 300° oven for 4 hours. Serves 6.

GOULASH

Goulash, like hash, has become a term to cover a multitude of dubious dishes, but a good Hungarian goulash does not warrant that treatment. When it is properly made, using the true Hungarian paprika pepper (accept no substitutes), it can hold its own with any fine stew. It is even better re-heated the following day than it is on the day it is made.

3 lb. chuck
3 onions, chopped
butter or oil
3 tablespoons Hungarian paprika (sweet)
2 1-lb. cans Italian peeled tomatoes, drained
2 green peppers, seeded and coarsely chopped
salt and pepper to taste
¼ lb. salt pork (in a thin slice)

Cube the beef. In an enameled pot, cook the onions over low heat in butter or oil until soft and discolored. Blend in the paprika, stirring constantly, and cook a minute or so. Add the beef, stirring it around to allow it to take on some color on all sides, putting up the heat slightly to do so. Add the tomatoes and peppers, season to taste, and cover with the piece of salt pork. Cover the pot tightly and over very low heat let simmer 2 hours, shaking the pot from time to time to prevent scorching. Serve with buttered noodles. Serves 4.

SAUERBRATEN

There are people who don't like sauerbraten, considering it too heavy, and I would admit that it is nothing you'd want to serve on a hot summer's day. But when the season is dark and the weather cold, when the wind cuts and the snow-laden clouds sullenly glare down, then I look to my wife's sauerbraten. This is how she does it—starting 3 days in advance.

> *3 tablespoons peppercorns*
> *1 tablespoon mustard seed*
> *25 cloves*
> *25 small bay leaves*
> *3 large onions, sliced*
> *2 cups wine vinegar*
> *3 lb. bottom round of beef*
> *salt*
> *6 slices bacon*
> *beef stock*
> *2 tablespoons flour*
> *¼ cup cold water*
> *2–3 tablespoons heavy cream*

Three days before you're going to serve this, combine the peppercorns, mustard seed, cloves, bay leaves, onion, and vinegar and pour it all over the beef. Keep in a cool place, turning it morning and night. When it has marinated for 3 days, preheat your oven to 400°. Drain the meat. In a dutch oven, casserole, or other oven-proof pot, place the meat and half the marinade. Add a pinch of salt and place in oven, uncovered, 1 hour. Then reduce heat to 300°, turn the meat, cover it with bacon and cook 1 more hour. Remove and discard the bacon and cook meat 10 more minutes. Now take the container out of the oven, remove and set aside the beef, and strain the liquid (a muslin dish towel inside a colander works well). Add to the strained liquid enough beef stock to make a total of 4 cups. Return meat to casserole, pour the 4 cups liquid and stock over it. On top of the stove, bring it to a boil. Blend the flour with ¼ cup cold water and add. Let it simmer 5 minutes, stir in cream, and serve. Serves 6.

OSSO BUCO

Osso buco is a speciality of Milan, a city that takes its eating so seriously that its citizens have combined dining with opera, serving full meals at La Scala during performances. (Berlioz complained that the clatter of silverware drowned out the music.) Being serious about food and agreeing on its method of preparation, however, are not the same. Waverley Root, in his authoritative *The Food of Italy*, reports consulting no less than 14 authorities on Milanese cooking about osso buco and coming up with no fewer than 14 different approaches. All did agree, however, that it was made with veal shanks. For this recipe, have the shanks sawn into 2- to 3-inch lengths, but have them of equal length and make sure they still have plenty of marrow.

5 *lb. meaty veal shanks cut into 2- to 3-in. pieces*
butter and/or oil
3 *carrots, peeled and coarsely chopped*
4 *stalks, celery, chopped*
3 *onions, peeled and sliced*
2 *cloves garlic, smashed*
½ *cup dry white wine*
1 *cup beef bouillon*
½ *teaspoon marjoram*

FOR SAUCE:
handful of chopped parsley
clove garlic, finely chopped
2 *cans anchovies, ground into a paste*
½ *teaspoon rosemary*
½ *teaspoon sage*
2 *teaspoons grated lemon peel*

Brown the veal shanks gently in butter (or oil and butter) and place on end in a large, flameproof casserole. Add carrots, celery, onions, and garlic and cook, covered, for 5 minutes over medium-low heat. Add wine and bouillon but see that the liquid does not quite cover the meat. Add marjoram. Simmer gently for 1½ hours. Five minutes before serving, combine and stir in the sauce. Serve with pasta or mashed potato or, most traditionally, Milanese rice. Serves 8.

TORTILLA CASSEROLE

Pre-Hispanic pottery figurines depicting women with metates—those specially shaped stones on which the tortillas are rolled out—suggest that the tortilla must be older than time itself. The addition of the cheese, which apparently was not made by the Indians, marks this as a more modern dish. The tortillas are best when fresh, of course, but both the canned and the frozen variety can do just fine and can be found in many supermarkets.

¼ cup oil
1 medium-large onion, chopped
2 good cloves garlic, finely chopped
1½ lb. ground chuck
1 1-lb. can Italian peeled tomatoes, drained
1 10-oz. can enchilada sauce
1 7-oz. (approx.) can sliced ripe olives
salt
pepper
8 tortillas
1 cup small-curd cottage cheese
1 egg
½ lb. jack cheese, sliced thin
½ cup cheddar cheese, shredded
tortilla chips

In a good-sized frying pan, heat up a little oil, then sauté the onions over medium heat until they take on some color. Add the garlic and crumble in the chuck. Blend in the tomatoes, then add the enchilada sauce and the olives with their liquid. Add salt and pepper to taste. When the mixture comes to the boil reduce heat and let simmer uncovered, about 20 minutes, giving it a stir every once in a while. Meanwhile heat the ¼ cup oil in a small frying pan until spitting hot and sauté the tortillas, one at a time, for a second or two on each side, or until they are just soft. Drain on paper towels and cut in half. Beat lightly together the cottage cheese and the egg. When the meat has cooked, grease a shallow 3-quart casserole and spread in layers first ⅓ of the meat topped with half the jack cheese, then half the cottage cheese, finished with half the tortillas. Repeat, using another ⅓ of the meat, then the remaining jack cheese, the remaining cottage cheese, and the balance of the tortilla halves. Spread with the remaining meat and top with cheddar and perhaps a border of crushed tortilla chips. Bake, uncovered, in a 350° oven for about 20 minutes, or until cheese is melted. Serves 6.

NEW ORLEANS GRILLADE

What makes this specifically "New Orleans" (even if it really is), I do not know. None of my family has any New Orleans connections (that I know of), but this recipe is one I can remember from youth.

    1 2-lb. slice of veal, about 1 inch thick
    oil
    2 large onions, sliced
    1 clove garlic, finely chopped
    2 green peppers, chopped

1 teaspoon flour
1 1-lb. can Italian peeled tomatoes, drained
1 pod red chili pepper
1 bay leaf
parsley
salt and pepper
1 cup hot water

Brown the veal in a small amount of very hot oil on both sides and remove from pan. Using more oil, if necessary, sauté the onions, garlic, and peppers until onions are soft and golden brown. Add the flour and stir around. Add the tomatoes, mashing them apart (the back of a slotted spoon works well). Cook, over low heat, 5 minutes. Add seasonings and meat and 1 cup hot water, cover, and simmer 2 hours.

NEW ENGLAND BOILED DINNER

This is corned beef and cabbage as it is served in New England. Most cookbooks advise you to cover the beef with water, bring to a boil, then drain, throwing out the first water. This is not always necessary. If the beef has been lightly corned, as is preferred in New England, the first blanching is superfluous. If in doubt ask your butcher, and if still in doubt, better blanch it.

4 lb. corned brisket of beef
4 white turnips, peeled and quartered
6 carrots, peeled and halved
6 potatoes
6 onions
1 cabbage, cored and quartered
6 beets (to be cooked separately)

Cover the beef with water and bring to a boil. If you are sure that blanching is unnecessary, proceed to let it simmer for 3–4 hours, otherwise pour off the water and begin again. When it seems nearly tender, skim off any scum that has formed (I find a tea strainer useful for this), and add the turnips, carrots, potatoes, and onions and let simmer, uncovered, 20 minutes. Add the cabbage and cook until cabbage is soft. The beets should be peeled and simmered in water about the same length of time as the turnips *et al.* (Don't cut the green part too close to the beet or it will "bleed.") Serve everything on a vast platter and if you have any leftovers, use them in a Red Flannel Hash (see next recipe). Serves 6.

RED FLANNEL HASH

This is the traditional aftermath of the traditional New England Boiled Dinner (see preceding recipe). You take whatever is left, *except the cabbage*, and chop it all up rather coarsely and mix it all together. Heat up some oil (or butter) in a heavy skillet and spread the hash on top. Cook it slowly, letting it get a good crust on the bottom. You can also "fake" a Red Flannel Hash, even if you haven't had the Boiled Dinner.

> 2 *teaspoons butter*
> 1 *onion, chopped*
> 1 *green pepper, seeded and chopped*
> 9 *medium-sized beets, diced*
> 6 *medium-sized potatoes, diced*
> 1 *lb. hamburger*
> *salt and pepper to taste*
> ¼ *cup water*
> 2 *tablespoons heavy cream*

Heat up the butter in a skillet and brown the onion and pepper until onion is pale. Add the beets and potatoes and the hamburger, season with salt and pepper, and add the water, stirring everything together. Let cook slowly, uncovered, on top of the stove for 45 minutes. Five minutes before removing from the heat, add the cream.

❦

CUBAN POT ROAST

This particular recipe is one that I married (yet another perquisite of the blessed estate). A notable aspect of it is the accompaniment, that typically Latin American combination, rice and beans. Don't be alarmed at using only half a green pepper in the pot roast—if you follow through on the rest of the menu, you'll use the other half in the black beans.

> *3 lb. chuck, in one piece*
> *salt*
> *1 clove garlic, mashed*
> *½ teaspoon oregano*
> *pepper*
> *2 cloves*
> *½ cup lemon juice*
> *oil*
> *½ green pepper, chopped*
> *1 onion, chopped*

Marinate the beef for at least 2 hours in the salt, garlic, oregano, pepper, cloves and lemon juice, turning it once. Then brown it on all sides over high heat in a little oil and remove. Into the pot put the pepper and onion, the meat, and then pour the marinade over it all. Cover and let simmer 2 hours. Serve with rice and Cuban Black Beans (see next recipe), for 6 people.

CUBAN BLACK BEANS

2 cups black (turtle) beans
5 cups water
pinch baking soda
2 bay leaves
pinch oregano
1 small jar pimentos, drained and chopped
½ green pepper, chopped
1 clove garlic, chopped
½ cup olive oil
3 teaspoons salt
pepper

Soak the beans for 6–8 hours in 5 cups water. Add the baking soda and 1 bay leaf. Bring to a boil, reduce the heat, and let simmer 1 hour, replenishing the water from time to time (the beans should be on the mushy side). Combine the other bay leaf, oregano, pimentos, green pepper, garlic, olive oil, salt, and pepper and let simmer 15–20 minutes in a small frying pan. When beans are almost cooked, add this to them and let simmer together 5 minutes.

TAMALE PIE

Here is a recipe with roots in the American West (or Southwest). It is an ideal party dish easily prepared beforehand and popped into the oven at the proper time. Although this recipe is for six, it can be doubled and redoubled to fill the largest casserole you can find—or several of them, although it is best to prepare the cornmeal-meat mixture in batches no larger than a double recipe. (Note also that a gargantuan pot will need more time in the oven —the "pie" should be liquid but not quite runny when tested.) As a final attraction, leftovers from the dish can be stored in the refrigerator for a day or so. Just add a little water (or tomato juice), sprinkle more grated cheese over the top and bake until bubbly.

> *1 cup cornmeal*
> *4 cups cold water*
> *2 eggs, well beaten*
> *1 cup olives, pitted and drained*
> *¼ cup oil*
> *1 lb. ground round*
> *2 onions, chopped*
> *1 clove garlic, finely chopped*
> *1 1-lb. can cream-style corn, drained (but save liquid)*
> *1 1-lb. can Italian peeled tomatoes, drained (but save liquid)*
> *3 teaspoons salt*
> *2 or more teaspoons mild chili powder*
> *¾ cup cheddar cheese, grated*

Add the cornmeal to the water and bring to a boil, stirring frequently. Once it boils, let it cook another 5 minutes, until mush is good and thick. Remove from heat and add the eggs, stirring thoroughly, and the olives. Set the mixture aside. Heat up the oil and when quite hot crumble in the meat and add the onion and garlic. Let cook, stirring, until meat has lost all its redness. Add the corn, tomatoes, salt, and chili powder. When mixture bubbles, taste for flavor, adding chili powder if necessary. Add enough of the tomato liquid (or mixed tomato and corn juices) to make the mixture quite liquid.

Ladle about a third of the cornmeal mush into a casserole, add a portion of the meat, and build up in alternating layers until everything is used up. Swirl once or twice with a fork or wooden spoon to distribute cornmeal evenly, but do not blend the two entirely. Sprinkle with the grated cheese and bake at 375° for 1 hour.

MRS. TREBLER'S POT

"The Swedish mother of a friend," writes James L. Steffensen, Jr., "served this at a birthday party when I was about 11. My brother and I demanded that our mother get the recipe. Mrs. Trebler obliged, and the Pot has since been a standby on both sides of the Atlantic, in kitchens whose equipment ranged from elegant wall ovens to one-burner hot plates. And it couldn't be easier."

> *oil*
> *1 lb. ground chuck*
> *1 onion, chopped*
> *1 clove garlic, chopped*
> *1 1-lb. can Italian peeled tomatoes, drained (but save*
> *   liquid)*
> *1 1-lb. can cream-style corn, drained (but save liquid)*
> *salt*
> *pepper*

Heat up the oil in an oven-proof dish or casserole large enough to hold everything, but not too large, and crumble in the meat. Add the onion and garlic and let cook, stirring, until meat has lost its redness. Add the tomatoes and corn. Combine the liquid from the two and add enough to make a slightly runny mixture (about 1½ cups) and add salt and pepper. Place the casserole, uncovered, in a 375° oven for 45 minutes. Check it from time to time, and if it seems too dry, add more of the liquid. It should be moist but not runny—but rather runny than too dry!

MOUSSAKA

Here is a dish that is found in a bewilderment of styles throughout the eastern Mediterranean. It is probably of Greek origin, although the Turks, among others, will certainly dispute the point. It is not a dish that you can whip up for an unexpected guest—it takes a certain amount of time. But much of the preparation can be done in advance, and if you have a large kitchen, you might invite your guests to help whisk the sauce. Otherwise time it so that the sauce is ready to go just as the guests arrive, and that will give you a good 45 minutes before the food is served. If your butcher cannot, for some reason, come up with ground lamb, buy some shoulder and grind it yourself, or use prepared lamb patties.

> 2½ *lb. eggplant*
> *oil, preferably olive*
> 2 *onions, chopped*
> 2 *lb. ground lamb*
> *salt and pepper*
> 1 *teaspoon ground cinnamon*
> 2 *1-lb. cans Italian peeled tomatoes, drained*
> 3 *tablespoons chopped parsley*
>
> SAUCE:
> 2½ *cups milk*
> 5 *tablespoons butter*
> 5 *tablespoons flour*
> *salt and pepper to taste*
> *pinch of grated nutmeg*
> 2 *egg yolks*

Peel the eggplant and slice thin, sprinkle with salt, and place in a colander topped with a weighted plate and leave to drain for half an hour or so. Rinse and squeeze dry with plenty of paper towels. Using just a little oil (the more you use, the more the eggplant will soak up), replenishing as needed, fry the eggplant lightly on each side and set aside on paper towels. In about 2 tablespoons of oil, fry the onion until just golden brown, add the ground meat and sauté until browned, then salt and pepper and add the cinnamon. Add the tomatoes and parsley and stir around well. Let cook over medium heat until most of the liquid has been absorbed. In an oven-proof dish that is higher than it is wide—and that is sufficiently decorative to be used as a serving dish—place a layer of eggplant, then a layer of the meat mixture, building up in layers but ending with a layer of eggplant. This can then be set aside while you make the sauce.

First heat the milk, but do not let it come to a boil. Then, melt the butter in a small saucepan and slowly, over low heat, add the flour, stirring (preferably with a small wire whisk) all the while. When it is well blended, slowly add the milk, stirring (or whisking) constantly. Season to taste with salt, pepper, and add the nutmeg, and let simmer until sauce thickens. Beat the egg yolks lightly, stir in a little sauce, then turn the egg yolks and sauce into the sauce slowly, still stirring. Pour the sauce lavishly over the eggplant and put the whole thing into a 375° oven for 45 minutes. Serves 6.

❦

LAMB AND APRICOT PILAFF

A factor in the cooking of North Africa and the Middle East—of Islamic cooking, if you will—is the widespread use of dried fruits in meat dishes. The apricots and raisins give this dish a savory taste that suggests the exotic. Although it's not strictly necessary, you may want to freshen the dried fruits by soaking them in warm water for the time it takes to brown the onion and lamb.

2 onions, finely chopped
½ stick butter
1 lb. boneless lamb, cut in 1-in. cubes

½ *cup dried apricots, halved*
3 *tablespoons raisins*
1 *teaspoon salt*
½ *teaspoon ground cinnamon*
pinch pepper
1½ *cups raw rice*

Brown the onion in the butter until it is soft and taking on some color. Stir in lamb and sauté until it all turns color. Then add the apricots, raisins, salt, cinnamon, and pepper, and about 1¾ cups water and simmer for an hour or so, or until the meat is tender. Meanwhile cook the rice the ordinary way. When the meat is tender, take a heavy pan and oil it well (or smear it with butter). Place a layer of rice and top it with a layer of meat, continuing until all is used up but ending with a layer of rice. Cover and cook, over the lowest heat you can contrive, for 25–30 minutes. Serves 4.

MOROCCAN LAMB STEW

In its place of origin, this might be made with lamb, mutton, or goat's meat. Lamb, of course, is used here; but if you're ever in a pinch, feel free to substitute.

4 *lb. leg of lamb*
¼ *cup olive oil*
3 *onions, chopped*
6 *cloves garlic, chopped*
ginger
parsley, finely chopped
salt and pepper
1½ *teaspoons saffron*
1 *1-lb. can Italian peeled tomatoes, drained*
2 *cups raisins*
1 *cup almonds*
butter

If you can get fresh ginger (vastly to be preferred) use a piece about the size of a walnut sliced thin; if not, use dried ginger, about a teaspoon and a half or so, and add with the saffron. Cut the meat off the bone and cube it. Heat some of the oil over high heat in a large pan and brown the meat a little at a time, removing it as it browns and adding just enough oil to keep it from burning as you do. After the meat has browned, in the same pan, but over reduced heat, sauté the onion, garlic, and (if you are using fresh) ginger. When the onion has taken on color, add the parsley and season with salt and pepper. Add the saffron (ginger, if you're using dried) and tomatoes and simmer about 1½ hours, or until the meat is tender (an old goat will take longer). While this is going on, soak the raisins in enough water to cover, and in a separate pan, sauté the almonds in butter, stirring all the time. Drain the raisins and add raisins and almonds to the meat and serve, perhaps crumbling hard-boiled egg over the top. If you can, serve it on a gaily decorated North African earthenware platter. Rice makes an especially nice accompaniment. Serves 6–8.

ADOBO

This is the "national dish" of the Philippines, where the taste of vinegar is highly appreciated. Since Philippine vinegar is less strong than what we are normally accustomed to, use a mild French vinegar and try the recipe a couple of times to find out just how much you like.

6 cloves garlic, mashed
2 chickens, cut in serving pieces
2 lb. pork butt, cut in 2-in. pieces
2 bay leaves

1 cup vinegar (or to taste)
salt and pepper
fat for browning

Mash garlic and put all ingredients together and let marinate overnight. Bring to a simmer in a heavy skillet and simmer until tender. Remove the pork and brown quickly in fat. Replace pork, heat, and serve. Serves 8.

LANCASHIRE HOTPOT

The British novelist Anthony Burgess extolls the virtues of this dish, which hails from the same part of England that he does. Like beef and kidney pie, it is best when cooked slowly, and also, like beef and kidney pie, it benefits from the addition of oysters.

2–3 lb. boneless lamb, cubed
2 onions, sliced
1½ lb. potatoes
¼ lb. mushrooms
½ lb. oysters, shelled
4 cups beef or chicken stock

At the bottom of a casserole that has a tight lid, place a layer of lamb, cover with a layer of onions, then a layer of potatoes. Repeat, topping with mushrooms and oysters. Add stock to nearly cover and place in a 300° oven for 2½ hours, covered. Serves 4.

❦

NANTUCKET FIREMEN'S SUPPER

This is appropriate for a party when you don't know when your guests will be ready to eat, for it thrives on long cooking. The dish was doubtless concocted just for that quality —firemen as a breed often finding themselves called out at inopportune moments and for unpredictable lengths of time, but in need of sustenance on their return. So long as this supper doesn't dry out (just keep adding milk) it simply gets better and better. Originally it was made on top of the stove in a soup kettle or similar utensil. It is even better made in the oven with the cover removed from its cooking utensil for the final half hour, to make the top crisp.

> 2 *tablespoons oil*
> 6 *pork chops*
> 4 *onions, sliced*
> 2 *lb. potatoes, sliced thin*
> ¼ *pt. heavy cream*
> *milk*
> *salt*
> *pepper*
> ½ *teaspoon thyme*

Heat the oil and brown the chops quickly on both sides. In the bottom of a greased oven-proof pot place the pork chops, cover them with a layer of onion, then cover the entire dish with the sliced potatoes. Pour the heavy cream over all and then enough milk just to cover and add salt, pepper, and thyme. Cover the pot and cook in a 300° oven for 4 hours (or longer). Check from time to time and add milk as needed. Serves 6.

BRAISED LAMB SHANKS

This is a favorite recipe of mine. Friends served the dish to me and from then on I intended to get their recipe. Somehow it kept slipping my mind or we had more important things to talk about or whatever. Finally I sat down one day and tested it out myself. One good meaty lamb shank should be plenty for one person. A fairly hearty red wine—a Rhône, a Spanish Rioja, or a Chianti—seems called for with it.

olive oil
2 lamb shanks
2 carrots, chopped coarsely
2 leeks (white part only), carefully washed and chopped
1 1-lb. can Italian peeled tomatoes
3 cloves garlic, finely chopped
2 bay leaves
½ teaspoon oregano
½ teaspoon thyme

Heat 2–3 tablespoons of oil in a skillet; wipe the lamb shanks with a damp cloth and then dry them well. Place in the hot oil and brown over high heat, seeing that they get browned on all sides and on top. Oil the bottom of a dutch oven and place all the vegetables and spices in it, mixing them around thoroughly. Add the liquid from the tomatoes. When the lamb shanks are well browned, place them on top of the vegetables, add a cup of water, and bring to a boil. Reduce the heat, cover, and let it simmer 2 hours or so, or until tender. Check once in a while to make sure water level isn't getting too low. This goes well with rice and a salad.

FEIJOADA

This is the national dish of Brazil, and if it boils down (as it were) to a marvelously augmented dish of beans and rice, that apparently is typical. According to Cora, Rose, and Bob Brown, the authors of *The South American Cookbook*, the Brazilian depends so much on these two commodities that instead of earning his bread and butter, he is said to earn his *feijao e arroz*—"beans and rice." In Brazil, again according to the book cited above, this dish would also include a smoked tongue and the ears and tail of the pig.

FEIJOADA
3 cups black (turtle) beans
¾ lb. dried beef
½ lb. smoked sausage
½ lb. smoked pork (or use smoked ham hock)
2 pig's feet
rice

SAUCE
2 tablespoons oil
1 onion
1 scallion
½ lb. fresh unsmoked sausage
1 clove garlic
cayenne pepper

Cover the beans with plenty of water and leave to soak overnight; at the same time, again in plenty of water, soak the dried beef overnight (much dried beef has some dreadful dye added to it and soaking gets it out). Drain the beef. Put all the meats excepting those for the sauce into a large pot, cover with fresh water, and bring to a boil, then reduce heat, cover, and let simmer. Put the beans and the water they soaked in into another pot. Check the water level, adding more if necessary to keep the beans covered. Bring them to a boil, reduce heat, cover, and let simmer. When the meats are almost tender (about 45 minutes) drain them and combine with the beans. Simmer another 15–20 minutes, or until beans mash easily. Make rice.

Heat up the oil and add the onion and scallion and mash into them the unsmoked sausage. Sauté gently until onions soften and take on color. Add the garlic and a pinch of cayenne and stir. Mash 1 cup of the beans into the sauce, moisten with some of the bean liquid, and let simmer 5 minutes; then turn the contents of the pan into the rest of the beans and meat. Stir well and simmer another 5 minutes. Remove the meat and slice it. Serve each person a slice of each kind of meat, put a little rice on the side, and cover the whole with beans. Serves 6.

❦

COUSCOUS

Couscous is a North African specialty and there are as many opinions on how to prepare it as there are North Africans—maybe more. It can be made with lamb or chicken or, if you're feeling expansive, both. Your true North African habitually eats it with a pepper sauce hot enough to bring the tears to your eyes and the sweat to your brow, which is fun for some and can be omitted by others. The couscous itself is a form of wheat called semolina, which in recent years has become available in specialty food markets, health food stores, and even some supermarkets. It can be made in a special steamer—a couscousière—or a large pot with a colander placed over it and is simply delicious. I like to serve it on an enormous serving platter with the meat in the middle, the vegetables on each side, and the grain heaped in a ring around them. It is the kind of dish that seems to lend itself to large, informal gatherings. This one should serve at least a dozen with something left over.

oil
3–4 lb. lean lamb, cubed
4 onions, chopped
6 oz. tomato paste
4 cloves garlic, crushed
1 1-lb. can Italian plum tomatoes
3–4 leeks, chunked
4 stalks celery, diced
2 carrots, coarsely chopped
1 teaspoon cumin
2 teaspoons caraway seeds
3 bay leaves
½ teaspoon coriander
1 lb. couscous
1 tablespoon saffron
½ cup raisins
2 medium green peppers, thickly sliced
2 large white turnips, thickly sliced
3 zucchini, thickly sliced
2 cans chick peas, drained
salt and pepper to taste
½ teaspoon cayenne pepper

Unless you have a heavy-bottomed soup pot, you're going to need about 6 ounces of tomato paste. In any event, wipe the meat and brown it in oil, taking the browned pieces from the fire and setting them aside. When all the meat is browned, brown *two* (or half) of the onions. If you are not using your soup pot for the browning process toss the browned meat and onions into the soup pot and add the tomato paste to the oil in the frying pan which you can then spoon into the soup pot. In any event, you should now have in the soup pot the browned meat and onions and any excess oil they were browned in (if you want to add tomato paste anyway, feel free). To the soup pot add the garlic, tomatoes, leeks, celery, carrots, cumin, caraway seeds, bay leaves, and coriander. Add enough water to completely cover the ingredients; cover the pot and bring it to a boil. When it does boil, turn down the flame and let it simmer a good hour.

While this is simmering, pour the couscous into a bowl and mix it around with your fingers to remove any lumps. Place the saffron in about one-half cup of hot water and set it aside to steep. Also put the raisins in a bowl of water to plump up (but drain them before adding them to the pot).

When the hour of simmering is up, add the rest of the vegetables, the chick peas, the (drained) raisins, add salt and pepper to taste, then add the saffron (with its water) and the cayenne. Mix the couscous around with your hands again, drain it, and place in a colander lined with a dampened piece of cheesecloth or muslin dish towel. Put the colander over the soup pot, but be sure that it is well above the liquid—if the couscous comes into contact with the liquid it will not steam properly. Cover the entire contraption and seal as tightly as you can (foil is a blessing here) and simmer another half hour.

SAUCE FOR COUSCOUS

2 tablespoons tomato paste
½ teaspoon paprika (domestic or Spanish)
¼ teaspoon ground coriander
up to 1 teaspoon hot cayenne pepper

To 1 cup of liquid from the couscous, add everything but the cayenne and stir around. Then slowly, tasting as you go, add the cayenne. When the sauce is hot enough to blow the top of your head off, it is ready.

HARIRA

If you ever have a Muslim friend drop by during the month of Ramadan and don't know what to feed him, this is the appropriate dish (at least to a Moroccan), but don't serve it until sundown. During that sacred month, the Muslim fasts from sunup to sundown, and clearly when the sun sets he is ready for something as hearty as this. The authentic meat would probably be lamb or mutton or goat (or camel, for that matter), but beef is acceptable. Pork is out. In the first place, it is forbidden to Muslims, and in the second it would probably taste awful prepared this way.

> ¼ *cup oil*
> *4 onions, sliced*
> ¾ *lb. meat (beef or lamb), cubed*
> *2 1-lb. cans Italian peeled tomatoes, drained*
> *3 carrots, chopped*
> *2 small white turnips, chopped*
> *1 lb. soup bones*
> *handful parsley, chopped*
> *1 tablespoon powdered ginger*
> *1 tablespoon saffron*
> *1 tablespoon Spanish paprika*
> *1 tablespoon black pepper*
> *salt*
> ½ *lb. lentils*
> *1 1-lb. can chick peas, drained*
> ¼ *lb. vermicelli*
> *4 eggs*

In a huge, heavy-bottomed kettle, heat up the oil and then add the onions and the meat and cook until the onions are soft and the meat has all changed color. Pour 2 quarts of water over the whole thing and add the tomatoes, carrots, and turnips, the soup bones, and the spices. Bring to a boil and add the lentils and chick peas. Let boil fairly vigorously, uncovered, and stir from time to time, for about 2 hours. Add the vermicelli (or rice) and let boil, less vigorously, for 20 minutes. Break the eggs into a bowl and with one hand pour them into the boiling brew while stirring madly with the other. Let simmer another 10 minutes and serve.

❦

CHOUCROUTE

This is a specialty of Alsace, and so an Alsatian dry white wine would seem the most appropriate wine to use and drink with it. A Sylvaner works exceptionally well, but a dry California white would probably do the job nicely. There seems to be some difference of opinion about sauerkraut. Some authorities say it should be rinsed to take out the strong taste—especially if it comes in plastic bags, in which case it may have been heavily sulfured. Perhaps it would be wise to taste the sauerkraut as you open it and see if you wish to wash it. Ideally, I suppose, you would make it yourself, but I've never tried that and have no advice for you.

½ lb. bacon
2 lb. sauerkraut
2 smoked pork chops (or smoked ham hocks)
2 fresh pork chops
3–4 cloves garlic, chopped
1 tablespoon juniper berries
2 bay leaves
2 cups dry white wine
pepper
12 allspice berries
2 tablespoons Kirsch
4 carrots, sliced
4 onions, chopped
½ lb. sausage

Line the bottom of a heavy, lidded pot with half the bacon, then add the sauerkraut, pork chops, garlic, juniper berries, bay leaves, white wine, a heavy grinding of pepper, the allspice, and the kirsch and top with remaining bacon. Bring it to a boil and let it simmer, covered, very gently for 3 hours. Add the vegetables and simmer 30 minutes more. Then add the sausage and simmer another 30 minutes. Crusty French bread and dry white wine are my accompaniments for it.

RABBIT AND LENTIL STEW

Americans have an odd outlook on rabbit. It seems to start with Flopsy, Mopsy, *et al.* and proceed via the Easter Rabbit all the way, perhaps, to the Playboy bunny. In fact, one major breeder of rabbits for laboratory use once fiercely denied that she would ever raise rabbits for food. Curious. On the other hand, rabbit breeder Mike Landress (whose rabbits are delicious) maintains that for their weight rabbits are the most efficient source of animal protein available. So reconsider, America! We can grow a lot more meat a lot more efficiently in rabbit hutches than we can on the vanishing range. However, if you want to be chicken about it, a good fowl makes an acceptable substitute for rabbit.

> *1 lb. lentils*
> *1 2–3 lb. rabbit, cut in serving pieces*
> *seasoned flour*
> *6 slices bacon*
> *3 onions, chopped*

2 *cloves garlic, finely chopped*
1 *green pepper, seeded and chopped*
2 *carrots, chopped*
½ *lb. mushrooms, sliced*
bay leaf
1 *teaspoon savory*
salt
pepper

Soak the lentils several hours or overnight in plenty of water, then put them, uncovered, on the stove and bring to a boil. Reduce the heat and let them simmer 30 minutes. They should be soft but not mushy. Preheat oven to 350°. Dredge the rabbit in seasoned flour and set aside. Fry the bacon until crisp and remove to absorbent paper to drain. In the bacon fat brown each piece of rabbit and set aside. Then sauté the onion, garlic, and pepper until onion is transparent. When the lentils are ready, combine all the ingredients, including the carrots, mushrooms, and spices, in a large, oven-proof pot and cook, covered, in the 350° oven for 1½ hours. Serve with sour cream.

BRUNSWICK STEW

In Colonial days this was made more often than not with rabbit or even squirrel, and today it can still be found made with rabbit. For some reason, we seem to have gotten away from cooking squirrel, although friends who have tried it assure me that it is delicious. The lima beans called for can be fresh, frozen, or dried; but if the latter are used, they should be soaked overnight and simmered for an hour

or so, until tender. I find it convenient to use frozen vegetables—2 packages lima beans and corn, 1 package okra.

> *1 slice smoked ham*
> *1 frying chicken or rabbit or two squirrels*
> *salt and pepper*
> *flour (for dredging)*
> *1 onion, chopped*
> *3 cups water*
> *1½ cups lima beans*
> *2 tomatoes*
> *⅔ cups okra*
> *1 tablespoon Worcestershire sauce*
> *1½ cups corn*
> *1 cup toasted bread cubes*

Cut the fat off a good slice of smoked ham and melt in a
frying pan or dutch oven (or use 4 tablespoons butter or
margerine instead). Skin and cut the meat into serving
pieces and dredge with salt, pepper, and flour. Fry the
chicken (rabbit or squirrel) and ham in fat until brown.
Add the onion and water, cover, and simmer until the meat
is almost tender (about 1 hour). Add lima beans, tomatoes,
okra, Worcestershire sauce, and corn, season, and simmer
until tender. Just before serving, stir in the bread cubes.
Serves 8–10.

LAMB STEW

To me, lamb stew will always be associated with the Ken-
tucky Derby, of all things. The best I can recall having was
served to a group of us who had congregated to watch the

running of the race on television and circulate a little currency among ourselves. I don't for the life of me know who won the Derby that year (*I* didn't), but I'll never forget the stew. This is as close as I've been able to get to it. If you wish to be elegant, use boneless lamb, about 2½ pounds, but I prefer the lamb with some bone in. Make sure you wash those leeks thoroughly!

4 lb. lamb
seasoned flour
2–3 tablespoons butter
1 qt. water
1 cup red wine
1 cup bouillon
2 bay leaves
1 teaspoon thyme
10–12 peppercorns
10–12 allspice berries
6 carrots, coarsely chopped
6 onions, chopped
2 leeks (white part only), chopped
3 stalks celery, chopped
6 small white turnips, peeled and chopped
6 potatoes, diced
2 cloves garlic, chopped
1 package frozen green peas

Cut the lamb up into small chunks and dredge it in seasoned flour. Using a large enamel pot or dutch oven, heat up 2–3 tablespoons butter, and slowly brown the lamb, removing the browned lamb to a platter or plate. When all the lamb is browned, put it all back in the pot and add 1 quart water, the red wine, bouillon, bay leaves, thyme, peppercorns, and allspice. Bring to a boil, cover, and let simmer 1 hour. Add all the vegetables except the peas and let simmer 30 minutes more. Add the peas, still frozen but separated from each other, and let simmer 10 minutes more.

BORSCHT

I would be hard put to define what a borscht is. What all borschts seem to have in common is an eastern European origin, beets, cabbage, and sour cream. Other than that, they range from soups to rich, meaty stews like this one, the borscht that is made by my wife. She thinks it had its origins in Poland, which her family left many years ago prompted by the sensible desire to avoid conscription into the Czar's army. With its special sweet-sour taste, it makes a fine meal, especially when accompanied by good, crunchy French or Italian bread and a simple green salad.

STEP ONE:
4 lb. beef chuck, cubed
1 lb. marrow bones
1 lb. smoked ham hocks
2 large carrots, unpeeled, in 1-in. chunks
2 onions, peeled but whole
1 stalk celery, with leaves
1 teaspoon salt
10 peppercorns
6 qt. water

STEP TWO:
8 tablespoons vinegar
4 teaspoons sugar
8 tablespoons tomato paste (about 1 6-oz. can)
8 tablespoons butter
1 lb. white turnips, peeled and cubed
1½ lb. yellow turnips, peeled and cubed
3 leeks (white part only), chopped
1 lb. carrots, peeled and chopped
1½ lb. cabbage, sliced
4 1-lb. cans cubed or julienne beets, drained

Combine all the ingredients marked for Step One in a soup pot and bring to a boil, reduce the heat and let simmer, gently, 2–3 hours, or until the stock has some bite. Skim off any scum. Remove everything except the beef with a slotted spoon. Cut the meat off the ham hocks and return the ham to pot. Discard vegetables and bones.

For Step Two, combine the vinegar, sugar, and tomato paste. In a goodly pot, heat up the butter and add the turnips (white and yellow), leeks, and carrots. Add the vinegar mixture and coat all the vegetables well with it. Simmer the vegetables for 25 minutes, then add the cabbage and simmer another 10 minutes. Now pour these vegetables and their attendant liquid into the meat and stock. Stir around and taste. If the sweet-sour balance is off, now is the time—and the only time—to correct it; use the same proportion of vinegar, sugar, and tomato paste—1 tablespoon vinegar to 1 tablespoon paste to ½ teaspoon sugar—in whatever quantity necessary. Bring to a simmer and cook until vegetables are tender; then add the beets and let cook until beets are heated through. Serve with plenty of good, rich sour cream. Serves 8.

6
Curry

Curries are curious things, if only that they are so hard to define. Aside from their being dishes of meat, vegetables, poultry, or fish that originated in the Indian subcontinent and are informed by Indian spicing, there seems little to define them otherwise. Indeed, one Indian cooking expert states that the only ingredient common to "all" curries in India is buttermilk (and also counsels those of us who don't have our own cow to use unflavored yogurt instead of commercial buttermilk). Many curry recipes do specify yogurt —sometimes as little as a tablespoon or so—but not all appear to do so. In a more innocent age it used to be thought that all you had to do was add curry powder and voilà. *Many of us today don't even have commercial curry powder in the house, and so even that won't wash any more. I suppose the best solution is to forget the definition and enjoy the food.*

One of the most common misconceptions about curry is that it is always seasoned with mouth-searingly hot spices. Not true. In fact, the chili peppers that pervade some of the curries served in the tropical south of India are not indigenous to the area at all. They were introduced from Central America in the sixteenth century. Some of the spices that pervade the gentler curries are cinnamon and cumin and turmeric.

LAMB CURRY

I usually use a small leg of lamb for this. However, it is important to remember that India for all her cultural richness is an impoverished country where neither people nor animals get enough to eat. Indian lamb, therefore, is *very* lean. So as you cut up the lamb, slice off all the fat, every bit. You can also peel the tomatoes if you wish. (Drop them in boiling water for a minute and they'll peel more easily.) I don't as a rule, and the dish seems to work out just fine. Or use a 1-pound can of Italian peeled tomatoes, drained.

> 6 *medium onions, finely chopped*
> 4 *tablespoons butter*
> 1 *tablespoon oil (preferably corn or peanut)*
> 2 *lb. lamb, cut in bite-sized pieces*
> 1 *tablespoon turmeric*
> 1½ *tablespoons coriander*
> 2 *teaspoons cumin*
> ¾ *tablespoon fresh ginger, finely chopped*
> 8 *oz. yogurt (or more, to taste)*
> ¼ *teaspoon crushed, hot chili peppers*
> 1 *teaspoon salt*
> 3 *large, ripe tomatoes*

In a heavy iron casserole brown the onions in the butter and oil (combined) until a deep golden brown (about 40 minutes). Add the lamb and stir mightily with a wooden spoon. Add the turmeric, coriander, cumin, and ginger. (Be sure to wear an apron here, turmeric stains—and badly.) Cook over low heat for 12 minutes, stirring constantly to keep from burning. It might be wise to keep a little extra oil handy in case either the lamb or the turmeric starts burning, in which case just add oil. Stir in the yogurt, chili peppers, and salt. Taking the tomatoes in one clenched fist (it's best to take them one at a time, naturally), squeeze them, crushing them into the meat. Bring the ingredients to a bubbly boil and cook down, uncovered, over high heat until the liquid is ⅔ gone and burning seems imminent. Reduce heat and cook another 35–40 minutes until meat appears solid, its coating about halfway between a paste and a glaze. Serves 4.

CHICKEN BIRYANI

Another Indian curry for chicken, this one works equally well with lamb. Again, it is well worth going out of your way to get fresh ginger, but if you simply can't find any, substitute a teaspoon of powdered ginger instead.

1 teaspoon coriander
½ teaspoon ground cloves
1 teaspoon cumin
1 teaspoon hot chili pepper
½ teaspoon cinnamon powder
½ teaspoon ground cardamom
½ pt. yogurt
juice of 1 lemon
3 cloves garlic, finely chopped
ginger (about the size of a walnut), finely chopped
1 2½ lb. chicken cut into serving pieces
4 onions, thinly sliced
oil
2 tablespoons salt
2 bay leaves
3 whole cardamoms
6 cloves
2 sticks cinnamon
2 tablespoons milk
½ teaspoon saffron
2 cups raw rice

Grind together the coriander, ground cloves, cumin, chili, cinnamon powder, and ground cardamom and place it in a large bowl with the yogurt, lemon juice, garlic, and ginger. Dry the chicken pieces and add them, turning them to coat them with the mixture. Sauté the onions in a little oil until golden and put ⅔ into the chicken mixture. Bring 4 cups of water to a boil with 2 tablespoons salt and the bay leaves, whole cardamoms, cloves, and cinnamon sticks and when it boils add the rice, stirring once with a fork. When it boils again, stir it once again, cover, reduce the heat and let simmer 5 minutes. Drain and spread out on a cookie sheet to cool. Heat the milk and add the saffron. In a large dutch oven, put first the chicken mixture and top with rice. Place remaining onions over it all and pour the saffron and milk over the whole. Bring to a boil and place in a 375° oven for 30 minutes. Reduce heat to 300° and let cook 30 minutes more. Serves 4.

CHICKEN KORMA

Not all curries are hotly spiced, so when a New York City food critic castigated an Indian restaurant for not spicing his korma hotly enough, he was reflecting a common misconception. Korma is a curry—but one that depends more on cinnamon than pepper. It is best made in a heavy-bottomed pan, such as enameled iron, and is served with rice.

MARINADE

4 *cloves garlic, pounded*
1 *onion, pounded*
1 *piece fresh ginger (about the size of a walnut),*
    pounded
pinch salt
1 *pint yogurt*

KORMA

2 *lb. chicken, cut in small serving pieces*
6 *cardamoms*
6 *cloves*
1 *teaspoon poppy seeds*
1 *teaspoon black mustard seeds*
4 *tablespoons butter or oil*
2 *onions, sliced*
1 *clove garlic, finely chopped*
1-*in. piece fresh ginger*
2 *tablespoons turmeric*
1 *tablespoon cumin*
2-*in. stick cinnamon*

For the marinade, pound the garlic, onion, ginger, and pinch of salt into a paste in a mortar with a pestle, then mix with the yogurt. Prick the chicken all over and let soak in the marinade for at least 2 hours, preferably 4. Also pound together the cardamoms, cloves, and poppy and mustard seeds. Heat up the butter or oil in your heavy-bottomed pan and brown the onion, garlic, and ginger. When they are brown, add all the spices and let cook for 2 minutes over low heat, stirring all the time. Then add the chicken and the marinade. Turn the fire up slightly to medium and let it cook until the yogurt has been reduced to a glaze, about 45 minutes. Stir it frequently to keep it from burning. If the yogurt has cooked down to a glaze and the chicken is done, serve it, but it's no disaster if the chicken isn't done. Simply add one-half cup of water, cover, and let simmer until the chicken *is* done. If your bird is so uncommonly tough that even then it's not done, add more water and simmer away.

CHICKEN TANDOORI

Although not perhaps technically a curry—what is?—this is a specialty of the Indian subcontinent, where it is usually cooked on a spit. However, it can be made in a regular oven as well. If you don't wish to keep a *garam masala* mixture (see page 128) on hand, grind together the following and use in its place: 1 teaspoon cumin, 2 teaspoons chili powder, 1 teaspoon salt, 6 peppercorns, 2 sticks cinnamon, and 2 or 3 cardamom seeds.

> *1 3–4 lb. chicken*
> *6 good-sized cloves garlic*
> *1 small onion*
> *1 piece fresh ginger (about the size of a walnut)*
> *1 cup yogurt*
> *1 lemon*
> *2 tablespoons garam masala (see above)*
> *ghee or butter or oil*

Skin the chicken but leave it whole. Chop the garlic and onion and ginger together, then place them in a mortar and with a pestle pound them to a smooth paste. Take your time with this. At first it will seem as though the onion will be your problem, but by the time you are nearly through, the onion will be a moist paste and there will still be small chunks of garlic left. Scrape them down from the sides of the mortar with a spatula or butter knife and keep after them. When the paste is finally smooth, add it to the yogurt and coat the chicken with it. Let the chicken stand in this mixture for 4–5 hours. One hour before placing chicken in the oven, squeeze the lemon and add to it the garam masala (or alternate mixture described above). Make a number of small cuts all over the chicken (to let the spices penetrate better) then spread with the lemon-spice mixture. Preheat oven to 400° and put in the chicken. Roast 1 hour and then baste with ghee or butter or oil (2 tablespoons). After the next half hour, baste with juices in the pan. Baste every half hour until done.

❦

SHRIMP CURRY WITH POTATOES

This one is fairly hot; so if you don't like hot curries, leave out the chili powder. If you do like hot curries, make sure you use a good hot chili—preferably Indian. I prefer using, as potatoes, the waxy red ones, and just scrubbing them well instead of peeling them. If the potatoes are larger in diameter than, say, 1¼ inches, you might want to cut them smaller than just into quarters. This recipe makes enough for two people if you are just serving it with rice and a salad, four if part of a larger spread.

> ¾ *lb. fresh shrimp*
> ½ *lb. new potatoes, scrubbed and quartered*
> 2 *tablespoons oil*
> 3 *onions, chopped*
> 1 *teaspoon salt*
> 1 *teaspoon garam masala (see page 128)*
> ½ *teaspoon turmeric*
> 1 *teaspoon ground coriander seed*
> ½ *teaspoon chili pepper*
> 1 *1-lb. can Italian peeled tomatoes, drained*
> *juice of 1 lemon*

Wash and shell the fresh shrimp and if there are several of you and the shrimp are large, cut them in half. As noted above, I like to keep the skins on my potatoes, but if they are old or you feel it is otherwise inappropriate, skin them. Heat up the oil in a large, heavy frying pan or dutch oven and let the onions get tender. Add the salt, garam masala, turmeric, coriander, and chili, stir it all together, and let cook over fairly low heat for 2–3 minutes, then add the tomatoes. (This operation is essential, although turmeric in a fairly dry pan tends to get into the air and irritate the nose—but don't worry, it ceases as soon as the tomatoes are added.) Mash the tomatoes down with a spoon until all is quite liquid, then add the potatoes. Let cook, stirring, about 5 minutes, then add a cup of hot water, bring to a boil, and let simmer gently for 15 minutes. Carefully stir in the shrimp, add the lemon juice, and let simmer 10 minutes more.

EGG AND MUSHROOM CURRY

Here is a good way of using up mushrooms that are threatening to turn bad on you. Unless they are very small, I would chop them coarsely. The coriander called for in the recipe is a standard ingredient of Indian (and Chinese) cooking, but sometimes hard to come by. Try substituting watercress leaves instead. Or in desperation, use parsley, preferably the Italian kind (also known as cilantro).

> *6 eggs*
> *½ lb. mushrooms*
> *oil*
> *2 onions, chopped*
> *1 piece fresh ginger, about ¼ oz., chopped*
> *½ teaspoon turmeric*
> *2 tablespoons fresh finely chopped coriander leaves*
> *2 teaspoons garam masala (see page 128)*
> *½ teaspoon hot chili powder*
> *1 1-lb. can Italian peeled tomatoes, drained*
> *2 tablespoons yogurt*
> *1 tablespoon lemon juice*

Hard-boil the eggs, then shell them and slice them length-wise into two and set aside. With a damp cloth or paper towel, gently rub each mushroom clean and set aside. Heat up a tablespoon of oil in a fairly large, heavy pan over medium-high heat and sauté the onion and ginger until onion is limp. Add the turmeric, coriander, garam masala, and chili powder. Stir and let cook 3 minutes. Add the to-matoes and the yogurt and mash it all together and let cook another 5 minutes. Add the mushrooms and let cook a minute or two, then cover the pan, reduce the heat slightly, and let cook 15 minutes. Carefully add the eggs (the yolks should not be dislodged from their nests), spoon-ing some of the curry over them. Let cook, covered, an-other 20 minutes, shaking the pan from time to time. Pour the lemon juice over it and serve with rice.

POTATOES AND SPINACH

Because so much of India is vegetarian, there has devel-oped there over the course of centuries any number of vege-table dishes using any number of combinations. This one may be a good dish to serve people who suffer the delusion that they don't like spinach. Small potatoes are best, and I prefer using the russet variety. In any event scrub them well—don't peel them.

½ lb. spinach
oil
1 small piece ginger, sliced thin
1 teaspoon turmeric
2 teaspoons salt
½ teaspoon hot chili powder
1½ lb. potatoes
1 teaspoon garam masala (see page 128)

Wash the spinach, then drain, chop fine, and set aside. In a large pan with lid, heat up the oil and then add the ginger and let it cook several minutes. Mix turmeric, salt, and chili well and add to ginger. (If you feel a tickle in the nose, that is caused by the turmeric.) Add the potatoes and stir around a minute or two, then cover and reducing heat, let simmer 15 minutes. Add the spinach and let cook, uncovered, another 15 minutes. The vegetables should be tender and the pan quite dry. Add the garam masala, stirring it around thoroughly, and serve.

❦

TURNIP PURÉE

This probably doesn't really belong in a book of mostly main dishes, but I include it here in deference to my editor, Bruce Carrick, whose taste for turnips is legendary. This dish also proved to me the futility of predicting what children will or will not eat. I had made some up one night when my two-and-a-half-year-old friend came over expectantly. "Knowing" that small children don't like spicy foods, I gave him a bite, figuring that would be the end of it. Hardly. He sat right there and matched me, bite for bite, until all was gone. Even so, it made a nice, light, hot-weather meal.

> 2 *lb. small white turnips, peeled and cut into small chunks*
> *1 tablespoon oil*
> *1 piece fresh ginger, sliced thin*
> *½ teaspoon chili powder*
> *½ teaspoon garam masala (see page 128)*
> *salt to taste*

Put the turnips in a small saucepan with water almost to cover and let simmer until completely tender, about 30 minutes. They should be fairly dry, but if they seem in danger of drying out before they are tender, add more water. When they are soft, mash them thoroughly. Heat the oil in a frying pan and slowly fry the ginger. Add the turnip and the other ingredients, stir it all together and cook it until it is dry.

DAL

One of the staples of the Indian diet is *dal*—the lentil. In India lentils come in a profusion of types whose gaudy reds and oranges and greens put to shame our drab brown ones. However, the ordinary lentil works well, too, and is much easier to find than, say, the pale green Moong Dal. Lentils are, of course, used in an endless variety of ways, one being as an accompaniment to almost any meal. Here is one way such a side dish might be prepared.

> *1 cup lentils*
> *salt*
> *1 tablespoon oil*
> *1 onion, thinly sliced*
> *small piece ginger, thinly sliced*
> *2 red chili peppers, or a pinch of hot chili powder*
> *¼ teaspoon turmeric*

Wash the lentils, then drain them and put them in a large saucepan with 2¾ cups water and bring to a boil, making sure they don't boil over. When they begin to boil, lower the heat, skim off any foam, throw in a pinch of salt and let simmer until dal is soft. Stir well. Heat up the oil in a frying pan and sauté the onion and ginger and chilies until onion is soft. Standing back to avoid getting splattered, carefully pour the contents of the frying pan into the dal and stir together. It goes well as a side dish with rice.

GARAM MASALA

This is the ubiquitous spicing of much Indian food and its precise quantities vary from home to home and from dish to dish. If you're going to be doing a fair amount of Indian-style cooking, it helps to have a jar on hand. Tightly closed it will stay fresh for months. Otherwise, use the slightly different individual spicing given in the recipe for Chicken Tandoori (page 122).

2 oz. peppercorns
2 oz. coriander seeds
1½ oz. caraway seeds
½ oz. ground cloves
20 cardamoms
½ oz. ground cinnamon

Measure everything out and place in a mortar, or preferably in an otherwise unused coffee grinder, and grind to a powder. Store tightly sealed.

7
Miscellaneous

PIPERADE

This recipe, for what is ostensibly Basque scrambled eggs, was supplied by MaryVonne Greenberg, who wrote home for it (home having been the French wine-growing district of Saint-Emilion, a hundred miles or so from the Basque country). It has the virtue of making an admirable brunch, giving you an hour or so to make inroads into the bloody marys or whatever. Just because the recipe came via Saint-Emilion, don't rummage around for your best vintage if you want a wine with it. Wine and eggs are uneasy companions at best and you'd do better to choose a lesser wine —possibly a rosé. While this recipe is for four, it can be expanded with ease. You will probably want to peel the tomatoes. I find it easiest to get a small pan of water boiling, stick the tomato with a fork, let it sit in the boiling water a minute or two, and the skin peels off like a charm. If you use two forks, you can be peeling one and softening up the next at the same time.

¼ cup olive oil
3–4 tomatoes, peeled and quartered
2 sweet green or red peppers, cut in thin strips
2 onions, chopped
1–2 bay leaves
2 cloves garlic, chopped
handful of parsley, chopped
salt
pepper
6 eggs
¼ teaspoon thyme

Heat up the oil in a large frying pan and throw in the tomatoes, peppers, onions, bay leaf, garlic and parsley. Salt and pepper lightly, cover, and cook over a moderate flame about half an hour. Uncover, increase the fire slightly, stir the mixture a bit, and let the liquid cook off, probably another 20–30 minutes. When the mixture has the aspect of a purée, beat the eggs lightly with the thyme, and pour over the vegetables. Cook, over quite high heat, stirring constantly for 3 or 4 more minutes, or until eggs are set.

❧

GERMAN POTATO SALAD

Potato salad has always been considered the *sine qua non* of summer picnics, but don't try this one for that. This one must be served hot and makes a splendid pickup on a blustery, raw, fall day. I prefer to use good-sized Maine potatoes—not Idahos!—for this dish. It also helps if you make your own chicken stock.

> 6 *potatoes*
> ¼ *lb. bacon*
> 1 *onion, chopped*
> ½ *cup chicken stock*
> ½ *cup vinegar*
> *salt*
> *pepper*

Cover the potatoes in a saucepan with water and bring to a boil, and cook them until the potatoes are cooked through but are still firm, not mushy. Peel them and slice them quite thin. Dice the bacon and put it over medium-high heat in a frying pan and let cook until it turns a delicate brown, stirring it around from time to time. Add the onion and let cook 5 minutes or so. Add the chicken stock and vinegar, a generous couple of pinches of salt and a good grinding of pepper, let it come again to a boil and then pour it over the potatoes. A sprinkle of chopped parsley adds a festive touch. Serves 6.

WELSH RABBIT

When I was a child, Sunday dinner was a formal meal usually served in the midafternoon, instead of at noon. This meant that supper was appropriately informal and more in the nature of a snack than a meal. Welsh rabbit was odds on the favorite Sunday supper. I don't usually serve it on Sunday evenings anymore, but it makes a fine Saturday lunch. It seems to work best with a slightly sharp New York State or Vermont cheddar, which melt more satisfactorily than processed cheeses seem to do and taste better too.

> *½ lb. cheddar*
> *2 teaspoons dry mustard*
> *½ can lager beer*

Cut the cheese into small cubes (or crumble it) and put it in a double boiler or saucepan with the mustard and the beer. Over low heat, stirring from time to time, let the cheese melt completely. Serve poured over toast.

CHEESE FONDUE

Originally a Swiss speciality that has spread to ski resorts the world over, classic fondue is made with one, or a combination, of four basic cheeses: Gruyère, Jura, Emmenthal, and Compté, with Gruyère and Compté usually used in the largest proportions. In some regions, mushrooms, slices of truffle, or other ingredients are added, but are generally thought to ruin rather than improve the fondue. In general, imported swiss cheese is to be preferred to "American swiss" or "domestic swiss," which often prove too fatty, resulting in a layer of oil on top of the fondue. The fondue is traditionally cooked over a burner on the table in an earthenware or enameled iron crock, and the wine used in its making is the best accompaniment. When the fondue has all cooked and been eaten, a brownish crust is left on the bottom of the pan. Known, for reasons unknown, as *la religieuse* ("the nun"), it should be pried loose with a knife and distributed to all who want it, for many consider it the choicest morsel of the dish. The following recipe is a per person recipe, to be augmented for however many more mouths you plan on feeding.

> ¼ *lb. cheese (especially Gruyère and Emmenthal, but also Jura and Compté if available)*
> *3 oz. dry white wine*
> *1 teaspoon flour*
> *pepper*
> *nutmeg*
> *1 tablespoon kirsch*
> *garlic*
> *French or Italian day-old bread in bite-sized pieces*

Either chop the cheese up into very fine pieces or grate it. Rub the bottom of the cooking pot with garlic and discard the garlic. Pour most of the wine into the pot (saving a bit to add later in case the fondue gets too thick) and heat it up. When the wine begins just bubbling, mix together the cheese and flour and add slowly and progressively to the wine, stirring constantly with a wooden spoon. When the cheese is all melted, add a pinch of pepper, a slight grating of nutmeg and the kirsch. Keep the mixture bubbling very slightly while you eat it, dipping the bread in with long forks and twirling it around to coat it with cheese. (Traditionally, dropping a chunk of bread into the pot costs the dropper a bottle of wine.)

RALPH'S SPAGHETTI SAUCE

Milly and Ralph Morrill live tucked away in the Adirondacks, near enough to New York City to make it a feasible weekend trip for friends escaping summer heat or, in winter, seeking the ski slope in the next town, with a result that no one ever really seems to know how many people are going to be around on any given weekend. One solution to feeding such a group is to skewer a goodly turkey with a felled sapling and let it cook, turning from time to time, over a charcoal fire. (It seems to work best if a light rain is falling.) Another is to break out the spaghetti sauce (which Ralph makes in vast quantities and freezes against need)— a maneuver that draws cheers from those fortunate to have had it before. Ralph stipulates Hunt's tomato sauce, not because he has stock in the company, but because Hunt's is the only one available in his area that advertises itself as unspiced. Ralph also feels that a good, cheap, fatty hamburger is called for.

2 *32-oz. cans Hunt's tomato sauce (or equivalent)*
2 *6-oz. cans tomato paste*
2 *tablespoons garlic powder*
oregano
6 *bay leaves*
Tabasco sauce
2 *lb. onions, coarsely chopped*
3 *cloves garlic, peeled and thwacked with the side of a
    knife*
1 *6-oz. can sliced mushrooms, with liquid*
2 *lb. hamburger*
2 *slices bread*
2 *eggs*
2 *cups red wine*

Pour the sauce and the tomato paste into a large, heavy pot with 1 tablespoon garlic powder, 6 tablespoons oregano, 6 bay leaves, and 6 drops Tabasco sauce, and bring to a low simmer. In a skillet, brown the onions and garlic over medium heat until translucent. Add the mushrooms and their liquid, 9 drops Tabasco and 6 tablespoons oregano and let simmer over a very low flame. Place the hamburger in a bowl and crumble the bread into it. Add the eggs, 2 tablespoons oregano, 1 tablespoon garlic powder, 3 drops Tabasco, and mix well. When the sauce and onion mixture have simmered separately for about 1¼ hours, add ½ cup red wine to the onion mixture and turn heat up slightly. Let cook 15 minutes, then add ⅔ onion mixture to the sauce, ⅓ to the meat. Rinse out the skillet and heat up ½ cup red wine. Add the meat mixture and stir it around over medium heat until it loses its redness (it will look very much like canned dog food). The meat can now be made into meat balls, doctored up with sausage or fennel or anything you like or it can be added to the sauce as is. The latter is what Ralph usually does, but before undertaking the operation, he carefully removes the bay leaves from the sauce. In such case, combine the meat and the sauce and let simmer, uncovered, for a few minutes until blended. As mentioned above, use what you need and freeze the rest.

SPAGHETTI ALLA CARBONARA

It is amazing how great a difference a pasta machine can make, but it is one of those things that cannot be described—only experienced. Most pasta lovers will tell you that once you have tried making your own pasta, you'll never—or only with the utmost reluctance—return to the commercial variety. If you don't make your own, use fettucine for this dish.

> *1 lb. fettucine*
> *6 slices bacon, diced*
> *3 eggs*
> *½ cup grated Parmesan cheese*
> *salt*
> *pepper*
> *parsley, finely chopped*

Cook the fettucine in a goodly amount of rapidly boiling, salted water, stirring from time to time, until just tender. Meanwhile, heat up the skillet and fry the bacon pieces until done, remove and let drain on paper towels. In a large bowl, beat the eggs lightly and add the cheese. Stir the eggs, cheese, bacon, and hot fat from the skillet together and add salt and pepper to taste and a tablespoon or so of parsley. Drain and add the fettucine, which should still be piping hot, and toss thoroughly. Serves 4.

TRIPE GENOESE STYLE

Tripe is the lining of a beef critter's stomach, a tough sheet of muscle that must be tenderized by long cooking before it is suitable for eating. In a rich country where meat is plentiful, such "by-products" as tripe are overlooked in favor of steaks, chops, and roasts. But as meat prices shoot up, more people are beginning to give more attention to the other parts of the animals we use for food. Tripe seems to be especially favored in Italy and France and both countries have evolved a number of ways of cooking it. Here is the Genoese way.

> 2 *lb. tripe*
> *oil and butter*
> *4 onions, chopped*
> *3 carrots, chopped*
> *3 stalks celery, chopped*
> *3 tablespoons dried mushrooms*
> *1 1-lb. can Italian peeled tomatoes, drained*
> *1 cup consommé*
> *1 teaspoon sweet basil*
> *salt and pepper*
> *potatoes (see recipe), peeled and sliced*

Put the tripe in a pan with plenty of water—no salt!—and bring it to a boil. Let it boil for 3 hours, then drain and cut it into inch squares. In a mixture of oil and butter, brown the onions, carrots, celery, and dried mushrooms and stir around, letting them brown until onion is limp and translucent. Add the tomatoes and the broth. Add the tripe, basil, salt, and pepper and stir it all around. Place enough slices of potato to cover on top, replace cover and set in a 350° oven for 30 minutes.

TRIPE À LA MODE DE CAEN

Caen is a small city in Normandy, a region known for its dairy foods and its apples. Cider is popular there, as is the brandy distilled from it—Calvados, the finest apple brandy in the world. Properly made and given a little aging, Calvados provides a heady spirit with an overwhelming aroma of fresh apple blossoms. Given its expense you probably wouldn't want to cook with it but use instead apple jack (an American apple brandy mixed with a goodly proportion of grain neutral spirits). Originally this rich, hearty dish was placed in a vast pot that was then sealed with pastry and carted off to the local baker to cook in his oven. Nowadays we have pots with tighter-fitting covers but fewer local bakers, so I don't bother sealing with pastry and I let it cook slowly overnight in my own oven. According to Escoffier, you can only get the proper consistency if you use an ox's foot—calves' and pigs' feet won't do! Even calves' feet are hard to come by these days, so use an ox foot if you can find one; otherwise substitute the calf or the pig.

    3 lb. tripe
    ½ lb. salt pork or slab bacon
    4 carrots, chopped
    4 stalks celery, chopped
    4 onions, chopped
    1 green pepper, chopped
    2 calf's feet, split
    cider
    ½ pint apple brandy
    3 cloves garlic, peeled and cut in two
    2 bay leaves
    ½ teaspoon marjoram
    ½ teaspoon thyme
    ¼ teaspoon mace
    1 teaspoon salt
    6–10 peppercorns
    6–10 allspice berries

Wash the tripe under fresh running water and drain. Cut it into squares of about an inch. Slice the salt pork or slab bacon and line a heavy, lidded dutch oven with the slices. Cover them with a bed of the vegetables, then add the calf's feet and the tripe. Cover it all with the cider and add the apple brandy and seasonings.

Place the cover on securely. If you're worried about the

fit of your lid, take a little flour and water and make a paste. Roll it out into a long "snake" and put around the top of the pot, then press lid down on it firmly. Place the pot in a 225° oven and cook 12–18 hours. To serve, ladle it out into soup bowls and have plenty of good crusty bread to sop up the remains. After the meal is the time to bring out the Calvados—not the apple jack.

Index